GERALD KINRO

A CUP OF ALOHA

THE KONA COFFEE EPIC

A LATITUDE 20 BOOK
UNIVERSITY OF HAWAI'I PRESS
HONOLULU, HAWAI'I

©2003 University of Hawai'i Press
All rights reserved

Printed in the United States of America

08 07 06 05 04 03   6 5 4 3 2 1

Library of Congress Cataloging-in-Publication Data

University of Hawai'i Press books are printed on acid-free
paper and meet the guidelines for permanence and durability
of the Council on Library Resources.

Designed by Kelly J. Applegate
Publication Services, Inc.

Printed by Versa Press, Inc.

CONTENTS

PART IV: A CUP OF ALOHA

INTRODUCTION

Coffee is one of the most extensively traded legal commodities in the world, ranking second to oil in the early twenty-first century. Coffee trading is a huge game that involves politics and price manipulation by the large producing countries. Kona coffee is a small subset of this vast output, representing a mere fraction of the world's coffee and grown in an area about twenty miles long and two miles wide. This strip that runs along Māmalahoa Highway in Kona Mauka (the mountainside of Kona) is known as the Kona coffee belt.

Kona, because of its minor status, has felt the undertows of coffee economics, both good and bad. It is subject to price swings and market gluts that have caused trying moments for the Kona coffee industry and Kona's tenders.

Historically, coffee took a backseat to the sugar industry in Hawai'i. Sugar took up most of the islands' agricultural resources with tremendous amounts of water, labor, machinery, and land going into its production. Sugar was a plantation crop with financial backing from large investors: AMFAC, Alexander and Baldwin, C. Brewer, Castle and Cook, and Theo H. Davies; they are collectively known as the Big Five. Most of the immigrants to Hawai'i came to work in the sugar industry; much of the population, therefore, has roots in sugar. Sugar reigned supreme for most of the twentieth century.

On the other hand, the production of Kona coffee has been a family operation. In times of economic downswings, all members of the coffee-growing family have had to bear the burden and work harder. Many times in its history, Kona coffee has been pronounced dead by experts. Nevertheless, each time Kona growers have managed to bounce back and stay alive. It took a special breed of person with a special kind of commitment to endure and to keep the industry going.

The irony of it all is that going into the twenty-first century, all but two sugar plantations in Hawai'i had been closed. The Hawai'i Commercial and Sugar Company (HC&S), owned by Alexander and Baldwin and Company and operating on Maui, was the largest. Kaua'i had a smaller plantation owned by the Gay and Robinson Company. Sugar, while still a major industry for Hawai'i, had been reduced.

Mirroring the decline in sugar production, Kona produced considerably less coffee than it had in the 1950s. Coffee did, however, outlast sugar on the Island of Hawai'i and entered the new millennium as a strong, viable industry. Many of its tenders diversified their operations as a safety net, and many farmed part-time. At any rate, challenges and price swings were present, even in the twenty-first century, and it took a strong will to keep it all going.

I got the idea for this story during one of my frequent trips to the Big Island. After seeing the one-time sugar lands along the Hilo and Hāmākua districts reduced to the production of macadamia nuts and other uses, with some lying fallow, I could not help but sense the irony of it all. One-time sugar barons were switching to coffee growing.

As I passed through Kahalu'u and Hōlualoa, Kona, I saw coffee trees, some of them fresh and new, while others were the same ones I saw as a youngster decades ago. They had survived. By the time I reached the Hōlualoa Japanese Cemetery, where my grandfather is buried, I felt a strong desire to read more about the efforts of those involved in Kona coffee. I wondered why someone didn't tell the story of Kona coffee. Although some work had already been done, there were areas upon which to be expanded. I recalled a lesson I had learned as a child: If you want something done, do it yourself. I knew that, true to the spirit of the Kona coffee warriors, I had to give my best effort in telling the saga of those whose efforts are best described as heroic. This is the story.

ACKNOWLEDGMENTS

Having grown up on a coffee farm, I thought I knew much about Kona coffee. I could not have been more wrong. This was certainly a learning experience. *A Cup of Aloha—The Kona Coffee Epic* could not have been accomplished without others providing support, information, artwork, and constructive criticism. So many people generously stepped forward to assist me in this project. I could not possibly name all who helped, but would like to acknowledge the following: Sam Camp of the Hawai'i State Department of Agriculture; Skip Bittenbender and C.L. Chia of the University of Hawai'i College of Tropical Agriculture and Human Resources; Warren Nishimoto of the University of Hawai'i Oral History Program; and Al Izen, Martha Noyes, and Waimea Williams for their invaluable criticism of the manuscript.

A special thank you to the following wonderful Kona people: Sotero Agoot of the Kona Pacific Farmers Cooperative; Sheree Chase and Terre Kriege of the Kona Historical Society; Richard Dinker, Ed Kise, and Tami Murakami of the Hawai'i State Department of Agriculture; Virginia Easton Smith of the University of Hawai'i Cooperative Extension Service; Dean Uemura of the Hawai'i Community Credit Union; Fujiko Akamatsu, Gladys Fukumitsu, Alfrieda Fujita, Steve Hicks, Ed Kaneko, Walter Kunitake, Herbert Okano, Norman Sakata, Leta Schooler, Bob and Cea Smith, and Vicki Swift.

I am grateful to editor Masako Ikeda and the rest of the staff and the reviewers at the University of Hawaiʻi Press for all of their constructive criticism and for believing in this work. Finally, I would like to thank my wife, Sandy, for her support and encouragement, and Dad, Mom, and my grandparents for getting aboard the coffee cycle. It was a great life.

PART I

·

ESTABLISHING AN INDUSTRY

·

CHAPTER 1

COFFEE COMES TO KONA

The Discovery of the Wonder Drink

Coffee's journey to Kona took hundreds of years and a roundabout route filled with luck, near misses, and legends. The journey began in Africa, where coffee's value as a stimulant was known centuries ago. Its earliest users ate its fruit and leaves. Nomadic warriors of Ethiopia's Galla tribe mixed crushed coffee beans and animal fat to create a meal high in protein and fat that helped sustain them on long journeys. Energy and caffeine made good food for soldiers, and the result was a fierce brand of warrior. During the late twentieth century, Ethiopian cookbooks contained a recipe for *Bunna Qela*—dried coffee beans—that mirrors the early preparation. Based on this evidence, it's possible that the practice of eating coffee may have been carried into the twenty-first century.[1]

Western legends credit an Ethiopian goat herder named Kaldi for discovering coffee's potent characteristics.[2] According to the tales, Kaldi noticed his goats in a frenzy after they had eaten the red coffee cherries. A curious sort, he sampled the cherries and was pleasantly surprised at the surge of energy he felt. He began dancing along with his goats. Soon, eating the coffee cherries became a daily habit. Kaldi's exuberant behavior could not go unnoticed, and an observant local monk decided to try the red fruit for himself. He, too, felt the surge of energy and decided to boil the fruits to make a drink to help other monks maintain their alertness during long prayer services. News of this super beverage spread, and soon all monks in the kingdom knew about coffee. The more enthusiastic monks indulged in the drink in order to allow them to spend a longer time in prayer.

The nation of Islam has its own version of coffee's origins.[3] They say that the angel Gabriel came in a dream to an ill Mohammed. The good angel showed Mohammed the red fruit and told him of its medicinal properties. It also had the power of stimulating the prayers of Mohammed's followers.

It is the Arabs who are associated with coffee's early cultivation and its use in the manner that we know today. The Islamic religion and coffee seem to have settled into the Arabian Peninsula at about the same time. After the fall of the Roman Empire and before the rise of Islam, the Persian army conquered Egypt and settled in the area. The Persians occasionally forayed into Ethiopia and returned with coffee to what is now Yemen.[4]

Arab medical books report the use of coffee at about the end of the tenth century. Originally monks drank coffee as an aid to keep them awake so they could pray. Its popularity spread among the population when many found that its use made average people "smarter." Because of coffee's popularity, special drinking areas— the first coffeehouses—were created. Despite opposition from religious zealots who considered coffee evil and advocated its ban, coffeehouses opened throughout the Middle East.

Spreading North—Kolshitsky, the Brave Innovator

The first coffeehouse in Constantinople opened in 1554, and by the seventeenth century coffee was a very popular beverage in the Arab world.[5] With the spread of Islam came coffee, which refreshed Turkish soldiers during their wars to expand their empire. Women got into the act of drinking this miraculous beverage, claiming it relieved the pains of childbirth. The rulers of the Ottoman Empire soon made the refusal of a man to provide his wife with coffee legal grounds for divorce.[6] It was a national drink and just as important as bread and water.

As the Turks conquered more territory, coffee challenged wine as the chosen beverage. Europeans who tasted coffee, however, found the beverage bitter and unpalatable. Although coffeehouses opened in London in 1650 and in Amsterdam in 1666,[7] it is Franz Georg Kolshitsky, a Pole, who revolutionized coffee consumption in Europe. First and foremost, Kolshitsky was a war hero to Austrians. In the late seventeenth century, Vienna was on the verge of being conquered by the Turks. Had the Turks succeeded, the area along the Danube River would have been cleared for further expansion of the Ottoman Empire. Kolshitsky is given credit for inspiring the Viennese to resist until the armies of Charles Martel could relieve them and defeat the Turks. The bilingual Kolshitsky took on the daring work of infiltrating enemy lines. It is during his spy missions that he tasted the miracle beverage and developed a liking for it. During subsequent battles, he collected booties of coffee from defeated Turkish army camps.

For his work, the grateful Austrians gave him total freedom in Vienna and a cash payment. Kolshitsky opened the first Viennese coffeehouse in the late 1600s and adapted his coffee to European taste buds by straining the grinds and adding honey and milk. Serving this new brew with crescents and doughnuts started the trend of pairing coffee with pastries and more importantly, drinking coffee became fashionable. Coffeehouses sprang up all over Europe, and coffee consumption increased. Traders who brought the beans back from the Middle East enjoyed much success.[8]

The Spreading of Seed

Coffeehouses came to the American colonies in the late 1600s. The beverage's popularity grew as the colonists protested the British tea tax.[9] At the time, however, the Arabian Empire was the only source of the bean. Arabian coffeegrowers were extremely protective of their plants and prohibited cuttings and seeds to leave their land. Baba Buddan, a Muslim pilgrim from India, smuggled seeds out of Mecca and planted them at his home in Mysore, producing the first coffee cultivated outside Arabia.[10] This escapade showed that coffee could grow beyond Arabia—and that it could be stolen.

In 1690 the Dutch, determined to earn their share of success from coffee's popularity in Europe, stole cuttings from Arabian coffee trees. These they transported to Java in the Dutch East Indies, where the Dutch established the first European-run coffee plantation. The plants thrived in this tropical climate, and the East Indies soon replaced Arabia as the world leader in coffee production.[11] The Dutch proudly showed off their success by exhibiting their Java-grown trees in the Amsterdam Botanic Garden. These trees became the source for the future of much of the world's coffee industry. The Dutch presented a single plant to Louis XIX of France in 1714. The gift was put into the Jardin des Plants in Paris, where it thrived in one of the royal hothouses under the care of botanists led by a Monsieur de Jussieu.[12]

It required the heroic efforts of Lieutenant Gabriel Mathieu Desclieux, a French army officer stationed in Martinique, to bring coffee to the Americas. An avid reader, Desclieux was aware of coffee's success in the East Indies. He knew that plants that did well in the East Indies also thrived in his West Indies home and concluded that coffee would do well in Martinique.[13]

He searched his home island for a plant fitting coffee's description but was unsuccessful. His interest in growing coffee stayed with him during his furlough to France. While there, he noted that all of the coffee consumed was from Arabia or the Dutch East Indies. This validated his belief that France should produce its own coffee.

Botanist Jussieu, however, would not share seeds or a shoot with Desclieux. Undeterred, Desclieux managed to persuade the king's physician-in-ordinary to give him a cutting. It was patriotic to do so, he said. He also obtained permission from the physician to export the cutting. All of this was unknown to Jussieu and the other botanists.[14]

In May 1723, Desclieux boarded a ship for his journey back to the New World, carrying his prized cutting in a glass case. It is said that the plant barely survived the journey. Desclieux awakened one day to find that someone had opened his glass case and broken a shoot off his plant. He feared irreparable damage and cursed himself for not being more vigilant. Desclieux suspected a Dutch spy, a person who spoke French with a Dutch accent he had encountered onboard. The alleged spy disembarked in Madeira.

There were other dangers as well. The French encountered pirates, and a fight ensued. Desclieux would not relent and protected his prize plant. They were on the verge of being defeated and taken over by the pirates and were rescued only when, by luck, a Spanish galley came to the area and assisted them. During the altercation, the cover to Desclieux's glass case was broken, exposing his plant. He considered keeping the plant wrapped in his cloak, but he decided it needed some light and did his best to repair the cover.

Then came a severe storm. This time the glass case was shattered and the cutting was doused with salt water. After the storm there came a windless period when the ship sat stranded in the Atlantic, and the hot sun beat down on the coffee plant, robbing it of much-needed moisture. The heat and the storm had nearly depleted the precious drinking water so necessary to sustain human life. Nevertheless, to save his coffee plant, Desclieux gave it his ration of drinking water. A thirst-crazed shipmate tried to destroy the cutting when he saw Desclieux watering it. The brave lieutenant fought the man off.

Finally the winds picked up, and the ship began to move. Still, the journey was a slow one. All water was used, and all aboard the ship lay weakly waiting for the inevitable, as there was no longer hope. Someone spotted land, however, and with revived energy, they sailed the last leg of their journey. They had reached the Antilles.

Desclieux and his cutting had survived, and it was planted in his Martinique plantation. This single tree produced the seeds and cuttings for many of the coffee plantations of Central and South America and, eventually, Hawai'i.[15] As for Desclieux, he became a Knight of the Third Order and, eventually, the governor of the Antilles.

Palheta's Patriotic Deed

The French and the Dutch controlled coffee production in the New World, maintaining plantations in French and Dutch Guiana, respectively. The Portuguese wanted a share of the production but were unable to obtain stock to start new plants in Brazil; both the French and the Dutch forbid the export of coffee cherries and cuttings.

Fortunately for the Portuguese, a boundary dispute erupted between French and Dutch Guiana. In 1727, a Brazilian envoy, Francisco de Melho Palheta, was called upon to settle the differences. While performing his diplomatic duties, he charmed and seduced the wife of the governor of French Guiana. Later, with the governor watching, his wife expressed her gratitude by presenting Palheta with a bouquet in which were hidden coffee cherries. Palheta dispatched these cherries to Brazil.[16]

Brazil became the world's leading producer of coffee, as well as the source of coffee planted in much of Latin America and the first coffee planted in Hawai'i and in Kona.

The Trip to Hawai'i—Boki Takes Charge

Don Francisco de Paula Marin—Chilean counsel and provisioner of ships, Kamehameha I's interpreter and physician, and distiller—planted the first coffee seeds in Hawai'i in 1817.[17] The flamboyant Marin was an avid horticulturist who introduced other plant species to Hawai'i and profited from the sandalwood trade. He also planted, in downtown Honolulu, the vineyards for which Vineyard Boulevard and Vineyard Street are named. His love for women is legendary, and he fathered at least twenty-three children. Marin perhaps undertook too much at one time, and coffee did not become established.[18] Nevertheless, he sparked further interest.

After Kamehameha I's death in 1819, his son Liholiho ascended to the throne to become Kamehameha II. At the time there were concerns of Russian influence in the islands. Kamehameha II (Liholiho) feared a Russian alliance with the chief of Kaua'i that could cause a civil war. Therefore, in November 1823, Liholiho and his wife Kamāmalu departed Hawai'i for England to ask King George IV to form an alliance for protection from the Russians. Among the members of Kamehameha II's entourage was Chief Boki, the governor of O'ahu.[19]

Sadly, it was on this state visit that the royal couple contracted measles, then unfamiliar to Hawaiians. Despite treatment by King George's physicians, the couple died, and Boki was left in charge of the delegation. He successfully completed Kamehameha II's diplomatic mission.

While in England, Boki visited several coffeehouses. He enjoyed them and the beverage they served. Seeing the potential for coffee to be grown in Hawai'i, he arranged to have the English agriculturist, John Wilkinson, come to Hawai'i to cultivate sugar and coffee in Honolulu's Mānoa Valley.[20] On the return trip, Boki had their ship, *H.M.S. Blonde,* stop in Rio de Janeiro, Brazil, to buy coffee seedlings for the project. In May 1825, *H.M.S. Blonde* arrived in Hawai'i.[21]

Wilkinson's efforts were more fruitful than Marin's, and he successfully established a coffee orchard. From this Mānoa field in 1828, Reverend Samuel Ruggles took cuttings and planted them near Nāpo'opo'o, South Kona, with visions of beautifying the area.[22] What Ruggles had done, perhaps without knowing, was to introduce coffee to an area ideal for its cultivation.

So a thousand years after its journey had begun and at the opposite end of the globe from Ethiopia, its ancestral home, Kona coffee lay in wait for its place in the sun.

CHAPTER 2

THE PIONEERS

The Slow Start

It was just a matter of time before enterprising Hawaiian business-men saw the economic potential of coffee. The first commercial venture in 1836 was not in Kona, however, but in Kōloa, Kaua'i. With Boki's Mānoa field supplying seeds and cuttings, Sherman Peck and Charles Titcomb subleased 400 acres to plant coffee, cotton, and mulberry for silk production. They did produce good quality coffee, but their main product, silk, failed. Therefore, the Kōloa company was dissolved.[1]

To encourage the production of coffee, the Hawaiian government in 1842 allowed the payment of land taxes in coffee as well as in pigs, which were a common means of payment at that time. The government also imposed a 3 percent duty on all foreign coffee imported into the kingdom, increasing this tariff to 5 percent in 1845.

In response to the government's policies, small acreages of coffee were planted in remote areas of O'ahu, Maui, and Hawai'i. The first large-scale coffee operation was started, again in Kaua'i, when Godfrey Rhodes and John Bernard planted 1,000 acres of coffee in Hanalei.[2] In 1845, the Hanalei company exported Hawai'i's first commercially grown coffee, a meager 245 pounds.

Coffee did poorly in the low elevations of Hanalei. Plants suffered from severe flooding and then a drought. A scale insect attacked the weakened trees. In addition, the California gold rush took needed laborers from the fields. Unable to continue, the defeated Kaua'i planters sold out in 1858.[3]

By then, commercial ventures had begun in Maui, Hilo, and Kona. In Kona, American and European growers found that coffee thrived on the slopes of Mauna Loa and Hualālai at about 800 to 1,700 feet above sea level.[4] This narrow area, just two miles long, was later to become the coffee belt. By 1870, areas outside Kaua'i, Kona included, were actively producing coffee beans. Kona coffee's quality enjoyed a boost courtesy of Mark Twain, who, in 1866, wrote in a letter to the *Sacramento Union:* "Kona coffee has a richer flavor than any other, be it grown where it may and call it by what name you please."[5]

It was sugar, however, that dominated agriculture in the islands at that time, assisted by a reciprocal trade agreement between Hawai'i and the United States. Huge fortunes were made as cane fields spread from the mountains to the sea. Growing, harvesting, milling, and shipping sugar involved a vast network of businesses and employed a substantial number of people. Sugar companies began getting contract laborers, first from China and then from Japan and the Philippines.[6]

Meanwhile, the outlook for coffee appeared bleak. The white scale severely damaged the failed plantation in Hanalei and threatened Hawai'i's entire coffee industry. Coffee in Kona was reduced to the upland coffee belt. American and European investors left, leaving native Hawaiians, who tended small parcels of land. The decline in Kona coffee was apparently rapid, for in 1866 Twain had reported that the groves of coffee in Kona were doing fine.[7] In a 1937 interview with Y. Baron Goto, John G. Machado, who arrived in Kona in the 1870s, about 10 years after Twain's visit, said that he found coffee uncared for and growing wild. According to Machado, the Hawaiians lived at the beach and went to the coffee fields only to harvest the crop. They carried bags of harvested coffee from the wild on their backs. Once in a while they would do some weeding.[8]

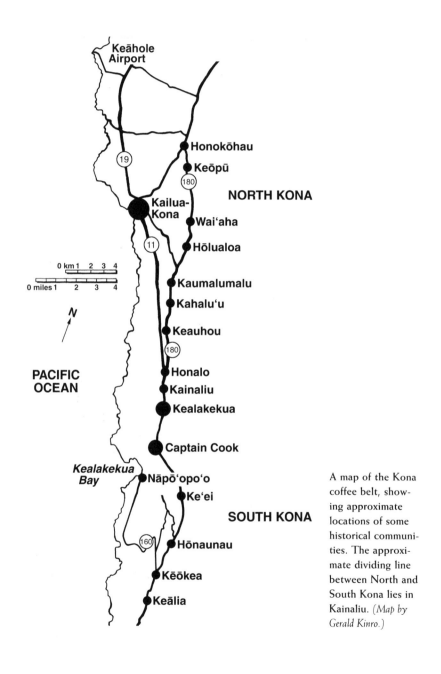

A map of the Kona coffee belt, showing approximate locations of some historical communities. The approximate dividing line between North and South Kona lies in Kainaliu. *(Map by Gerald Kinro.)*

During the late 1860s and early 1870s, the reputation and good prices that Kona coffee had enjoyed in the San Francisco market declined. According to Machado, the decline was due to improper processing. The Hawaiians, he said, had no training or equipment to process coffee properly. Machado built the first coffee processing mill in Nāpō'opo'o and purchased coffee from the Hawaiians, paying them with merchandise.[9] This kept Kona coffee going, but despite Machado's efforts, coffee's future did not look good.

In the 1890s, several events helped save the coffee industry in Hawai'i. The first was the introduction of the Australian ladybird beetle, which successfully controlled the white scale. Second was the sad overthrow of the Hawaiian monarchy in 1893. The new provisional government opened up lands to be leased for coffee production in the hope of encouraging Caucasian settlers to grow coffee. The third factor was the sharp rise in world coffee markets. This fueled the expansion of coffee and inspired more Caucasian businessmen to invest in it. These investors planted coffee on all major islands. As a result, plantations such as the Kona Tea and Coffee Company in North Kona were established.

Nineteenth-Century Kona Pioneers of Importance

In addition to John Machado, there were other European and American planters who gave Kona coffee a start in the late nineteenth century. In North Kona, there were Dr. A. McWayne, F.W. Bartels, George McDougal, N.F. Scott, and Emil Mueller. In South Kona, there were J.F. Morgan, F.B. McStroker, Robert Wallace, J.M. Monsarrat, W.B. Castle, and J.B. Castle.[10]

There are, however, four pioneers in the development of the Kona coffee industry who stand out. These four left the greatest lasting impressions on the industry. The first is Charles D. Miller of the Kona Tea and Coffee Company. Honolulu investors owned the company, but Miller, an Englishman by way of Ceylon, managed the operations.[11] He employed many Japanese laborers who later became farmers. Miller's legacy is one of information; he brought to Kona knowledge about coffee culture that he put into practice and shared with others. He would later introduce to Kona the coffee variety that would carry the Kona name.

W.W. Brunner, a German immigrant, planted coffee in South Kona. During the boom period of the early 1890s, he converted his pineapple cannery into a coffee mill.[12] This act gave impetus for the further growth of Kona coffee. He would later be instrumental in the transition from coffee-growing plantation to family-owned farms.

Robert Robson Hind, a British immigrant, had become successful in the sugar business in the Kohala District.[13] During the boom period of the early 1890s, he moved to South Kona to grow coffee. He subsequently purchased J.B. Castle's interest in the Captain Cook Coffee Company, which included a processing mill.[14] By 1910, the company controlled 1,200 acres of coffee lands and owned three coffee mills.[15] As a processor and landlord, the Captain Cook Coffee Company was a major player in the Kona coffee story until the middle of the twentieth century. After Hind's death, the management of the company and its holdings went to his son John.

Arguably the most illustrious of the four pioneers is Henry Nicholas (H.N.) Greenwell. A native of England, Greenwell left his homeland in the 1840s to seek his fortune. His exploits took him to Australia, where he planned to raise sheep, but a drought ended his plans. Next the California gold rush beckoned the 24-year-old. Knowing prospectors needed supplies, he set off with provisions. His crew, however, caught gold fever, leaving him to unload the ship alone. He injured his back, and because doctors in California also had a passion for gold rather than for medicine, Greenwell went to Honolulu for medical attention. He arrived in 1850, after the Great Mahele that allowed the private ownership of land. The enterprising Greenwell moved to Kona, where he began buying land and tried several agricultural ventures, including sheep and oranges. He established a general store in Kealakekua.[16]

H.N. Greenwell, a nineteenth-century exporter of Kona coffee, was recognized for his excellent coffee at the Kaiser's Exposition during the 1873 World's Fair in Vienna. *(Courtesy of Steve Hicks, Greenwell Farms.)*

As a coffee exporter, Greenwell developed a reputation for the consistent good quality of his products. This quality was due to his selectivity in purchasing his products for market.[17] In 1873, Greenwell was recognized for his excellent coffee at the Kaiser's Exposition during the World's Fair in Vienna.[18] At a time when the reputation of Kona coffee was on the decline, he maintained a standard of excellence, which left a permanent imprint on Kona coffee.

The Move Toward Family-Owned Farms

With rising coffee prices, Portuguese laborers moved to North Kona to work in the coffee fields. In 1892, Japanese immigrants began to settle into Kona to work for the Kona Tea and Coffee Company.[19] This growth was short-lived, however, and prices soon fell as dramatically as they had risen. With prices plummeting, investors turned elsewhere. Coffee plantations disappeared throughout Hawai'i and were replaced by more lucrative sugar fields.

For coffee, all that remained were the crops in Kona and those in a small area in Hāmākua on the other side of the island. Kona's terrain was too steep and rocky for sugar. The slopes of Mauna Loa and Hualālai could never support the new machines that were coming to serve the sugar industry. Sugar eventually went out of cultivation in Kona.

The land in Kona was, with its friable volcanic soil and good drainage, suited for coffee cultivation. The climate in Kona also was made for coffee growing, with a cool, dry season from November to March. This creates a dormant period in the coffee plant that synchronizes the opening of buds with the rains that come during spring. Rainfall is heavy during the spring and summer months, when the fruit is maturing. This leads to high-quality coffee and high yields. Furthermore, Mauna Loa and Hualālai attract afternoon clouds that shield the coffee plants from the intense direct sunlight, further enhancing the quantity and quality of the crop.[20] Kona and coffee were a perfect fit.

By this time some of the coffee workers had developed an interest in farming on their own. Many took this opportunity and leased land from the Bishop Estate, the largest private landowner in Hawai'i, and other landowners for fees ranging from $300 to $1,000 per farm. The financial position was difficult for these Japanese farmers; they had no income yet from their crops because it takes four years after planting for a coffee crop to be produced, and they still faced the expenses of tending their farms.

Sanshichi Ozaki, a Honolulu businessman; Kenji Imanishi, the manager of the Honolulu branch of the Yokohama Specie Bank; and Consul Miki Saito negotiated with the Japanese government to release $10,000 of contract laborers' unclaimed savings still in the custody of the Honolulu Branch. This release helped subsidize some of the Kona coffee growers.[21]

Another significant, but often overlooked, event in Kona coffee history is O'ahu grower Hermann Widemann's 1892 introduction of a coffee variety that evolved in Guatemala. Until then, Kona's cultivars were the progeny of plants brought from Brazil by Wilkinson and Boki. This variety was called "Hawaiian coffee," or *Kanaka koppe*.[22]

Widemann's friend John Horner planted 400 seedlings of the *Kanaka koppe* and 400 of Widemann's newly introduced variety in his Hāmākua orchard to compare their performance. By 1895 Horner was convinced of the superior quality of the 'Guatemalan' variety. Miller introduced the 'Guatemalan' variety to Kona, obtaining seeds from Horner and planting them in Kona Tea and Coffee Company's nursery in Kahalu'u, North Kona. Miller left before his seedlings were ready for transplanting, however, and Zentaro Inaba continued Miller's work, planting the seedlings in Wai'aha, North Kona, in 1897. (Inaba later built and ran the famous Kona Hotel in Hōlualoa.) In a major planting, Kunigoro Yokoyama in 1899 planted 100 acres of 'Guatemalan' in Kaumalumalu, North Kona, with plants grown from seeds he purchased from Horner.[23]

By 1910, other Kona growers were sold on the 'Guatemalan' variety and had made the switch. It was to become known as *Meleken koppe,* or "American coffee." With the emergence of the term *specialty coffee* in the 1990s, some began calling this variety "Kona typica" to avoid confusion in the market between coffee

A tree of 'Guatemalan,' or "Kona typica," the standard-bearer of Kona coffee. *(Photograph by Gerald Kinro, 2001.)*

This 1931 family portrait shows Kunigoro Yokoyama, one of the early planters of the 'Guatemalan' variety of coffee, seated in front of his store in Kaumalumalu. *(Japanese-American National Museum. Gift of Gladys [Yokoyama] Fukumitsu.)*

from Guatemala and the popular Kona coffee variety known locally as 'Guatemalan.' At any rate, 'Guatemalan' became the standard-bearer for Kona's coffee industry.[24]

W.W. Brunner provided the chance for independence for some coffee growers. With coffee prices dismal in the early 1900s, Brunner sublet 100 acres of coffee farmlands under a sharecropping arrangement. He provided housing and a water tank. His compensation was one-third of the growers' yields. With prices remaining low, Brunner subsequently sold his interests to the Captain Cook Coffee Company, which charged growers rent for the land and bought all of what they produced.[25]

More farmers arrived in Kona. Although the influx was multiracial, it was primarily the Japanese who moved from the plantations into independent business ventures.[26]

The work was hard and the profits small, but gone were the indignities of working for a *luna* (overseer). Although most farmers were eager to escape the harsh, almost brutal conditions of plantation life and be their own bosses, some emigrated.[27] Whatever their individual reasons, coffee growing was not for the weak.

Kazo Tanima, born November 13, 1893 in Japan, had an adventurous spirit and a sharp business mind to go along with his agricultural skills. As a young man, Tanima had thought of going to Hawai'i, but his father cautioned him against the scheme, citing Hawai'i's lack of young women. But his father later summoned him to Hawai'i, where the elder Tanima worked on a sugar plantation. Tanima arrived in 1912 and worked in Lāhainā, Maui.

The young Tanima found plantation life not to his liking. The overseers were Portuguese and Hawaiian, and he could not communicate with them. Instead, he chose to become an independent contract cane grower. He excelled and made a good profit. He then planned to go to Wahiawa to work in the pineapple fields, but a friend told him that one could grow anything in Kona. Tanima took his friend's advice and arrived in Kona on December 22, 1915. A few months later, on April 16, 1916, Tanima purchased a coffee farm with his earnings. He was determined to succeed, feeling that if others could do it, he would try.[28]

Waichi and Kame Okano came to Kona partly for the adventure and partly for the money. Kame Okano, born on February 9, 1889, in Yamaguchi Prefecture, Japan, disliked farming as a girl. She wished to live the life of a storekeeper. One of her cousins was married into the Okano family, and they took her in. When one of the Okano sons, Waichi, returned from the Japanese-Russo War, he had visions of coming to Hawaiʻi. He needed a wife to make the move, and Kame's sister offered Kame, and so Kame and Waichi were married.

Kame wanted to come to Hawaiʻi, thinking it would be a good place. The Okanos planned to stay in Hawaiʻi for 10 years, earn money, and then return to Japan. They chose Kona because a neighbor was already in Honalo, North Kona. They arrived in Hawaiʻi in 1907. After a brief stay in Honolulu, they arrived in Nāpōʻopoʻo, the only passengers on a cargo ship. In Nāpōʻopoʻo they found only Portuguese and Hawaiian wagon drivers who spoke no Japanese. After much searching, they finally found a Japanese driver. The fare to Honalo was $4.50, but they did not have the money. They shook their purse and were still 10 cents short; the driver agreed to waive the 10 cents.

In Kona they lived at several locations. Waichi did weeding on several coffee farms. Kame picked coffee. She picked a bag a day, earning 50 cents per bag. Later, she worked in the sugarcane fields and then at a tobacco farm, clearing weeds. After earning enough money, the couple purchased a seven-and-a-half-acre coffee farm in Honalo. They later moved to Keauhou.[29]

The Tashima family became coffee farmers because of misfortune, not by intention. Originally from Kumamoto Prefecture, Japan, they settled in North Kona in 1914 after years of living and working on a sugar plantation in the Kaū District. Like most Japanese who came to Hawaiʻi as contract laborers, they planned to return to Japan. After 10 years on the sugar plantation, they had the money they needed and were about to move back to their homeland.

However, patriarch Uichiro Tashima heard of opportunities in Kona. He decided they needed just a little more money. He worked in sugar in North Kona. Wealth did not come, however. Instead, the family returned home one day to discover that their hard-earned savings had been stolen. This sealed their fate, forcing them to stay in Kona and eventually farm coffee.[30]

The Filipinos were the second largest group of newcomers. Like the Japanese, they came for independence. Many first worked as harvesters and then became independent farmers. Two of the early pioneers from the Philippines were Francisco and Agustina Alvado, who came to Hawai'i in 1916 to work in the sugar fields. The Alvados eventually moved to O'ahu and opened a tailor shop. They were moderately successful, but then hard times struck.

A friend told them about Kona's opportunities. It was a nice place with no boss for whom to work. They decided to make the move, and their friend brought them to Kawa'aloa, South Kona. They purchased five acres from the Machado family, who owned a general store.

They were spirited, brave, and willing to learn. As Agustina told an interviewer with the Oral History Project of the University of Hawai'i: "We had no experience in coffee farming. We looked at what others were doing and learned." They sold their crop to Machado.[31]

Through hard work and often primitive farming methods, an industry was born. Kona had 273 Japanese coffee growers in 1909. By 1914, nearly 4,000 acres were cultivated. By 1931, more than 1,300 families grew coffee on 5,500 acres. They owned an impressive 2,448,000 trees,[32] and they produced 9,808,000 pounds of green coffee beans.[33] Where corporate efforts had failed, family-run enterprises had survived and kept Kona coffee alive.

PART II

■

SETTING THE STAGE

■

THE PLAYERS AND THEIR ROLES

Like all dramas, the Kona coffee story has its cast of characters. Appropriately, the characteristics of the coffee grown in Kona and the growers' commitment to quality played major parts in the creation of these roles.

First, coffee grown for commercial production is made up of two major species: *Coffea canephora* and *Coffea arabica*. *C. canephora*, known to some as "robusta coffee," is strong and disease-resistant and competes favorably in harsh ecosystems with relatively little care. Its high caffeine content, however, makes it bitter, and its high acidity has a souring effect. Therefore, despite the advantage of hardiness, coffee from *C. canephora* is of poor quality.[1] Produced in large quantities in Africa and Southeast Asia, it is sold as a blend to lower prices or as low-quality canned coffee.

C. arabica is the species grown in Kona. Unlike its hardy relative, it requires intensive care. *C. arabica* is susceptible to drought and other adverse weather conditions. It cannot resist disease. Weeds can rob this plant of needed nourishment, rendering it unproductive. It thrives only in near-ideal ecosystems and only with constant nurturing. Its lower acidity and caffeine content make it more palatable than *C. canephora*. Furthermore, the intensive care required for *C. arabica* production adds to its quality and the flavor that coffee drinkers love. These needs created the role of the care-giver or farmer.

Second, coffee in Kona begins to ripen in August, but all fruits on a tree do not mature at the same time. There are green, or immature, cherries among the mature fruit. Ripe coffee cherries produce the best coffee, and immature fruits compromise quality.[2]

The easiest way to harvest the coffee cherries would have been to imitate the Brazilians, who stripped the trees bare, taking a crop only once instead of hand-selecting the ripe fruits. In Kona, however, a standard for quality had been set and only ripe cherries were picked. The race was on to get the crop harvested before it fell to the ground or was destroyed by the rats.

From the early farmers onward, this meant work for the entire family. It meant rising before dawn and heading to the fields and working until sundown. The routine continued seven days a week until the season ended.

Harvesting was systematic. The harvesters picked every tree in every line, every line in every plot, and every plot on the farm. Then they repeated the cycle to pick the cherries that had ripened since the prior harvest. A family usually completed four or five cycles in a season that lasted from August until January. In most cases, the plot just picked would ripen before the completion of the round and demand attention. To keep up, farmers relied on members of the second group, the pickers.

Another characteristic that shaped the characters in the drama is the process required to convey coffee to the consumer. Coffee is not a commodity—such as an apple, a tomato, or an egg—that can pass directly from the farmer to the consumer. It requires several steps of processing before it is consumable. Although coffee cannot be improved once harvested, improper processing can ruin the coffee, allowing fermented juices to spoil the taste of the bean.[3] Therefore, in Kona they processed the beans as quickly as possible.

Harvested cherry coffee. *(Photograph by Gerald Kinro, 2001.)*

The easy way of processing the beans would have been to employ the dry method, in which the harvested coffee cherries are dried and then the extraneous layers that surround the coffee bean are removed in a single step. This method is fast and efficient but produces coffee of inferior quality.

The wet method of processing takes more time and labor and is more costly, but it yields coffee of better quality. The wet method involves two stages: wet processing and dry milling. Wet processing begins with the removal of the thick, leathery pulp that covers the harvested coffee beans. The harvested cherries go into a pulper that removes the outer skin without crushing the bean. The depulped beans have a slimy mucilage covering that, in Kona, is removed by fermentation. During fermentation, the depuled beans must sit in water as bacteria eat away the slime. Then the beans are washed clean and spread on a flat surface for drying. The dried product is called *parchment coffee*.

The dried parchment coffee must then be dry milled to remove the parchment and the thin, silvery film that covers the bean. The product after dry milling is known as *green coffee*.

The green coffee is graded, separating flat from round beans and then separating the beans according to size. Stones, shells, and immature beans are removed. Finally the coffee is sorted by color. Green coffee is then roasted, ground, and now ready for consumption.

In the final stage of wet processing, parchment coffee is spread to dry. *(Photograph by Gerald Kinro, 2001.)*

Green coffee ready for roasting. (*Photograph by Gerald Kinro, 2001.*)

Machado observed nineteenth-century Hawaiians in Kona using the dry method or a partial wet method of processing. Those using the partial method removed the pulp by spreading the coffee cherries on a large *poi* board and *jerking* a stone about the size of a coconut over them. The pulped coffee was then dried without removing the mucilage. To get to the green coffee, the Hawaiians placed dried coffee into a stone or wooden container and pounded it with a cylindrical stone about fourteen inches long, three inches in diameter at the base, and slightly tapered at the top, where it was held with both hands. If the quantity of coffee was large, they used a wooden hammer supported by a beam and operated with the feet, a *kimo laiki*. According to Machado, coffee processed this way was of poor quality because most of the coffee beans were broken.[4]

Since the late 1800s, Kona coffee has been processed using the wet method. Many small farmers did their own wet processing; many did not. Until the late 1900s, very few farmers, if any, did dry milling. Therefore, this need for processing of harvested coffee created the role of miller.

Rounding out the cast are the landowners and the store owners. We can now examine the individual roles in more detail.

Farmers

For many of the immigrant farmers, the freedom they sought was an illusion. Farming on their own was better than plantation life, but there were still many restrictions placed upon them. Although the work was hard, it was not unexpected. Other factors made life difficult.

First, farmers were subject to economic downswings. These downswings destroyed coffee operations owned by larger entities in other parts of Hawai'i and constantly pressured Kona farmers. Even in good times the Kona farmers were constantly aware that bad times could arrive without notice. They were always prepared to switch, at a moment's notice, to survival mode. Insecurity was a basic condition.

Changes in the weather could have catastrophic results. A lack of rain could produce a poor harvest or even kill producing plants. Other pests wanted their share of the crop. Although the white scale disease that ravaged the industry in the 1860s had been dealt with, rats that harbored in the *Pandanus* and other trees common in Kona's farmsteads devoured the ripe coffee cherries while they were still on the trees. The introduction of the ladybird beetle to control the white scale and the halo fungus is an example of a successful biological control effort. The importation of the mongoose to control rats is an example of a failure. The nocturnal rats and the diurnally active mongooses never met. Before the use of anticoagulant rodenticides, farmers set traps. They collected the rats' tails, and their children were paid 2 cents apiece for them at school—a significant contribution to the family's income.

Another obstacle was that many farmers had no knowledge of coffee growing, having arrived fresh from a sugar plantation. Although experienced as agricultural laborers, they now owned businesses and needed management skills as well. They knew little about marketing and markets, the economy, and other factors necessary for success.

Land in Kona was scarce. Farmers had to lease acreages and, therefore, were easily manipulated. Most early farmers had minimal savings, and many relied on credit for daily essentials, giving power to the lenders. In addition, most knew little, if any, English. Few had connections outside their communities. Therefore, farmers rarely set their own prices, relying on buyers to give the best deal. It was usually a take-it-or-leave-it situation. Those in Kona took it. With no connections, little formal education, and little capital, they had to or return to the plantation.

Pickers

Pickers were independent individuals who moved from farm to farm much like the itinerant laborers described by John Steinbeck in *The Grapes of Wrath*. Pickers were different from *mahina men*, permanent laborers who, in addition to harvesting, helped with other chores during the off-season and often lived in separate quarters on the farm.

Some pickers lived in Kona, holding other jobs during the off-season, while others were migratory and came from other communities on the island. Many were Filipinos. Some were single, while others were married and brought their families to help. "*Osan,* you need pickers?" was their familiar refrain when approaching a farm with an abundance of ripe cherries. They were always welcome.

One such picker was John Santana, born in Kohala, Hawai'i, in 1906, the son of Puerto Rican immigrants.[5] He recalled going to work with his father to hoe weeds on the sugar plantation while still a boy.

He came to Kona as a coffee picker in the 1920s, when the going rate was 50 cents per bag. Since he could pick only a bag a day, he earned 50 cents for a full day's work. After the season, he took on contracts to clear weeds from lands. He used his cunning nature to earn more by going only to farms with an abundance of ripe cherries, where picking would be easy and profitable. He became more adept at his craft, and his earnings increased. He eventually purchased his own farm in Kahaluʻu, North Kona.

Severo Dinson was born in Cebu, the Philippines, in 1904 and learned of opportunities in Hawaiʻi from a cousin. He arrived in Hawaiʻi penniless and was assigned to the Pāpaʻaloa plantation in the Hāmākua district. Workers there told him he could earn more by picking coffee in Kona. In 1927, he made his move. Dinson found picking easy and could harvest ten bags a day. In 1928 the rate was $1 a bag. It rose to $1.25 per bag, then fell to 40 cents a bag in the 1930s.[6] In a span of a few years, Dinson saw his earnings cut in half.

As a single man, Dinson was mobile and traveled the island to wherever there was work during the off-season. He also made money as a prizefighter. He eventually married and settled in Kona.

Landowners

Most farmers could not afford their own land and had to lease their farms. The landowner had much control over the farmer. The Bishop Estate was the major landowner in the Kona area. Also of note was the Captain Cook Coffee Company. After purchasing interests from Brunner, the original landlord of many of the farmers, the Captain Cook Coffee Company became the leaseholder for these farmers. The Captain Cook Coffee Company kept control of its lessees through their rental agreements. Leases stipulated that the farmer was to sell all of his coffee back to Captain Cook. With few other options and out of fear, the farmers complied.[7]

Other landowners were George Henriques of Nāpoʻopoʻo and Sherwood Greenwell, a descendent of H.N. Greenwell, who leased land in Kealakekua and Nāpoʻopoʻo. Sherwood Greenwell considered his lessees independents, as they were able to sell their produce to whomever they wished, unlike lessees of the Captain Cook Coffee Company.[8]

H. Hackfield and Company, renamed American Factors and later AMFAC, was one of the few coffee-processing options farmers had in the early 1900s. Kailua-Kona, 1909. *(Japanese-American National Museum. Gift of John Weeks, courtesy of the Reverend Shugen Komagata.)*

Millers

In the late 1890s and early 1900s two companies did the bulk of the coffee milling: the Captain Cook Coffee Company and H. Hackfield and Company. The latter became American Factors and then AMFAC. Because the Captain Cook company wet-processed coffee, it purchased newly harvested cherry coffee from the farmer. American Factors purchased only parchment coffee that it dry-milled. With no other outlets, early farmers were forced to sell their products to these two entities at low prices.[9] So powerful were these companies that at one time the Captain Cook

Coffee Company and American Factors controlled 80 percent of the coffee lands being farmed.[10]

To remedy this, the Japanese organized their own coffee mills. The first was the Kona Coffee Mill Company, which was formed in 1899.[11] This company offered growers cash payment and higher prices. Still, obtaining coffee from growers was difficult, as many were obligated to either Captain Cook or American Factors and feared that breaking of any agreement would have dire circumstances. Therefore, the Japanese company set up *midnight coffee runs* to pick up coffee without detection from the two big companies.[12] They called this bootlegged coffee *nukashi*. There were, however, remaining concerns of detection, as many farmers feared they were being watched. "American Factors would hire a guy to patrol the highway at night," said Minoru Inaba, son of Zentaro Inaba, the early planter of 'Guatemalan' coffee.[13]

The Japanese company did not turn a profit until the early 1920s, when it switched from an association to a corporation. With this new organization, the Kona Coffee Mill Company was finally able to repay its entire mortgage to the Bank of Hawai'i.[14] It operated until the Great Depression.

During the 1920s, more Japanese began to open their independent mills. The Kona Coffee Mill Company was the training ground for Minoru Tanouye, who managed the mill for a short time in the 1920s. Born on the Hāmākua Coast in 1892, Tanouye came to Kona at age 6 and was raised by an uncle. He worked for a sugar company until 1923, when he went to work for the Kona coffee company as a hired hand. In 1924, the company's manager resigned, and Tanouye was hired to manage the mill at $75 per month. He later worked in conjunction with the Wing Coffee Company in Honolulu. Wanting more, Tanouye started his own coffee mill in 1941 and began his own brokerage.[15]

Another Japanese miller was Yoshio Noguchi. Noguchi was born in 1907 in Maui and moved to Kona in 1916 when his father decided to farm coffee. In 1928 Noguchi and several friends started

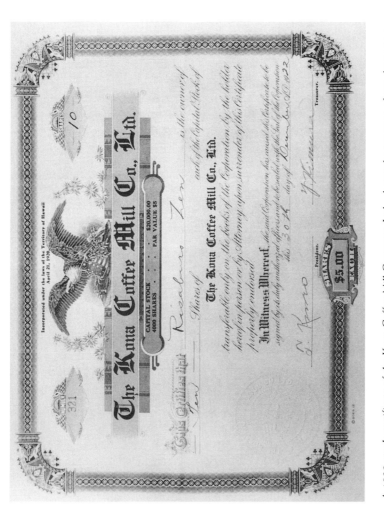

A 1922 stock certificate of the Kona Coffee Mill Company, Ltd., shows the issuance of ten shares to a Risaburo Zen. (*Japanese-American National Museum. Gift of Alfrieda Fujita, courtesy of the Reverend Shugen Komagata.*)

Four members of the Kona Japanese Association, organizers of the
Kona Coffee Mill Company, are shown together in the early 1920s.
Community leader Harvey Saburo Hayashi is seated on the right.
Standing at left is Tatsutaro Kinro, president of the mill during and
soon after its incorporation in 1920. *(Hatsue Kinro collection.)*

a mill that went bankrupt in two years. Undaunted, he formed his own processing company. He initially sold his coffee to the Captain Cook Coffee Company. Nevertheless, he claimed to give growers better prices than Captain Cook or American Factors would have. He later got an agent in New York to assist him in marketing.[16]

By 1940, there were eight Japanese-owned coffee mills in Kona.[17] Through their own dealings they were able to sell coffee to their own sources and offer cash payment to their farmers. Nevertheless, American Factors and the Captain Cook Coffee Company reigned supreme into the 1950s.

Stores

Store owners were intermediaries between the farmers and the landowners and between the farmers and millers. Although the Captain Cook Coffee Company leased farmland, both it and American Factors controlled the distribution of goods—food, clothing, and other supplies—that the farmers needed to survive through the network of the many stores along the belt highway. Because many farmers had no cash, American Factors and Captain Cook Coffee Company, through these stores, extended credit to the farmers by supplying them with necessities for living and farming. The farmer would repay his debts with coffee he grew, again through these stores. This system made both American Factors and the Captain Cook company all the more powerful and profitable. They were in a position to make demands.

This credit system was one of the reasons for the abundance of small general stores in the villages of Keōpū, Hōlualoa, Kaumalumalu, Keauhou, Honalo, and Kainaliu in North Kona, and Kealakekua, Captain Cook, Kealia, and Honaunau in South Kona. Some of them were less than a minute's walk from one another. The coffee belt at one time had as many as forty stores along its twenty-mile length—one store for every half mile.[18] When considering that Kona's population, until the 1960s, was less than 10,000 and was made up primarily of farmers, this is a substantial number.

The stores, with soft drink and cigarette posters giving them their characteristic appearance, carried a little bit of everything. Kunigoro Yokoyama, the early planter of 'Guatemalan' coffee, sold "Dry goods, Boots, Shoes, Hats, Japanese Provisions, Groceries, Hardware, Crockery, Cigars, Tobacco, and Japanese Drugs."[19] Some store owners kept a pool table in the corner for workers to enjoy a game after work. Some cut hair.[20]

Stores were an important place for socialization. Virtually all stores had a bench in front, and there often was a group sitting outside talking. The owners' families often lived above or behind the store. They grew coffee, tended vegetable gardens, and kept hog pens nearby.

Usaku Morihara used the profits of his frugal investments to start the Morihara Store in Hōnaunau, South Kona, in 1924.[21] He also became a coffee broker. As owner of the Sun Mellow Coffee Company, he borrowed money and, in turn, used it to make loans to farmers in need of cash. He took payment in coffee. He made cash purchases for coffee from growers who were not indebted to him. Morihara sold his coffee to a dealer in Maui.[22]

Sun Mellow closed when Morihara was interned during World War II along with others of Japanese ancestry. His store continued to operate, however, and continued after his return. It was sold in 1995, and the establishment entered the twenty-first century with another owner who renamed the business Merv's Place.[23]

Another Important Role

Many of the accomplishments of the Kona farmers were the result of Harvey Saburo Hayashi, a nonfarmer. He was born in 1868 to a poor *samurai* family in Fukushima Prefecture, Japan.[24] His father wanted him to become a physician, and he enrolled in the Aomori Medical College. Although Hayashi graduated with honors, the school was second-rate, equivalent to a junior college. The young Hayashi, therefore, hoped to continue his education in the United

States and eventually in Germany, the mecca of medical education at the time. Against the wishes of his father, Hayashi left home at age 18 to prepare for his journey abroad. He chose San Francisco because of the influence of the Japanese Gospel Society in that city.

Hayashi left for San Francisco with spirits high but cash low. While aboard ship, he asked the ship's captain to hire him as a cabin boy because he needed money. The captain took an interest in Hayashi and honored his request. He also taught Hayashi conversational English.

Life in San Francisco was not easy. Hayashi took a job as a houseboy for a wealthy family while attending high school at night. In school, he studied English and took pre-med courses. A year later he left his domestic job to become an itinerant fruit picker. During his days on the farms, he experienced firsthand the prejudices Japanese workers encountered. These experiences helped shape the ideals that would eventually take him to Kona.

He continued his schooling and graduated from the Hahnemann Medical College in San Francisco with highest honors. His professors called him "Harvey" after the British anatomist and physiologist William Harvey. During this time, he became a close friend of the Reverend Jiro Okabe, who left to do missionary work in Hilo, Hawai'i.

Hayashi practiced in California but did not like the racial prejudice that was predominant at that time. Plus, he still had dreams of continuing his medical education in Germany and then going back to Japan. Fate had other plans, however. He received a request from Okabe to come to Hawai'i to practice. Hayashi decided to join Okabe and to save some money before moving on. He opened a practice in Honomū, a plantation town just outside Hilo.

While in Honomū, he saw the oppression the Japanese plantation workers faced. In addition, they lacked proper medical care that most could not afford. Hayashi abandoned his dreams of gong to Germany and of returning to Japan. Instead, he felt it was his Christian duty to serve a poor area of Hawai'i considered undesirable or unacceptable by other physicians.

He arrived in Hōlualoa, North Kona, in 1895.[25] As the only physician of Japanese ancestry in Kona he provided invaluable health care to the community for more than 40 years, often with no compensation. His contributions to the farmers, however, far exceeded the range of his stethoscope.

As a community leader and activist, Hayashi fought for the rights of poor coffee farmers. He helped establish the Kona Coffee Mill Company to give farmers better prices. A believer in education, he helped start the Japanese language school and organized the Japanese Language School Association. He kept farmers informed through his Japanese language newspaper, *The Kona Hankyo* (The Echo of Kona). Hayashi's role in the Kona coffee story, although tangential in appearance, was certainly an important one and touched the lives of every farmer in the district.

CHAPTER 4

LIFE ON A FAMILY COFFEE FARM

Waichi and Kame Okano, the couple who arrived in Kona in the early 1900s with a meager $4.40, shared their living space with bags of coffee parchment. Still, Kame Okano considered the room that was twenty feet by forty feet large. "Ten people slept in there," she said.[1]

It was in this room that she gave birth to ten children. Waichi was the midwife who heated water over a wood fire, poured it into a washtub, and delivered his children. The Okanos typified the independence of the coffee farmers who learned and practiced the skills to survive. In doing so, they built their farms to provide for themselves.

A Culture of Self-Sufficiency

Farms averaged between two and fifteen acres. A coffeehouse for habitation was an unpainted wood structure with a metal roof. A veranda cooled the home. Many of the early twentieth-century homes had rock walls with wooden tops and corrugated metal roofs. There was no concrete to hold the stones together. A home of about 500 square feet housed the entire family.

In both the rock-walled homes and coffeehouses, the kitchen and dining areas had dirt floors. In the absence of appliances, a *kudo* (wood fireplace) served as a stove. In an article written for the

Honolulu Star Bulletin in 1938, Koji Ariyoshi, son of a coffee farmer, painted a dismal view of living conditions on the farm. "Kitchen walls were black with soot from smoke. Children read before fireplaces or work at repairing coffee baskets and patching torn coffee sacks. The whole family sleeps in one room. Houses had no ceiling and galvanized roofs leaked."[2]

While dining the family typically sat on wooden benches. The sleeping area had a raised wooden floor. There were no beds, and the family slept on mats, or *futons*. Kerosene lamps lit the house during the evening, providing the only illumination for children to do their homework.

With no wells or municipal water systems, a wooden water tank with a capacity of about 10,000 gallons served as the family's main

A *kudo*, or indoor fireplace, used for cooking before the arrival of appliances. Photo taken at the Kona Historical Society's Living History Farm. *(Photograph by Gerald Kinro, 2001.)*

source of water. Originally, families brought water from the tank into the home with pails. Plumbing evolved as farmers, with some of the profits earned from their labors, installed pipes from the tank to the "kitchen." To supplement the water supply, farmers put out metal rain barrels throughout their farms. Those who wet-processed their coffee had additional water demands and often had a second tank.

A drought could send water levels dangerously low and be damaging to the tank, as the outward pressure exerted by the water of a full tank was important to maintain its shape and utility.

With this limited amount of water, conservation was vital, even in times of plenty. There were no opportunities for long showers. Each home had a *furoba,* or bathhouse, separate from the living area. The *furo,* or bath, was a wooden vat with a copper bottom. Its water was heated with burning wood. Baths were taken in the Japanese fashion, with washing and rinsing done outside the *furo,* and the bath used only for soaking after one was cleansed. Water had to be stretched for several days and then fed to thirsty plants.

Howard Tatsuno, a teacher at Konawaena High School, recalled tanks being contaminated by insects, dead rats, and bird droppings and wondered how people managed to survive under such unsanitary conditions. A tobacco bag on a faucet served as the only filter. Still, he recalls no one becoming ill.[3]

Jean Yoshida Matsuo recalled the pleasures of feeling the softness of water from her tank as she filled her cupped hands and took a sip. She and her family, during a downpour, put out available pots and pans and tubs to capture the rain. Like most from Kona, Matsuo considered this cool, refreshing water a priceless gift from heaven.[4]

With no refrigeration, food was stored in screened wooden cabinets called *safes.* Food items that were stored were the least expensive, easy to prepare, and nonperishable; many were grown on the individual farms. Typically, each farm had fruit trees—papayas, mangoes, avocados, breadfruit—and a vegetable garden. The leaves

Coffee farmers raised chickens for eggs and for meat. *(Circa 1947 photo from the Gerald Kinro collection.)*

of the Spanish needle (*Bidens pilosa*) and the popolo plant (*Solanum americanum*) were eaten as vegetables, as were bamboo shoots. Farmers raised chickens for eggs and for meat, feeding them leftovers and letting them loose to forage. They also raised hogs, which were fed cut grass, avocados, and papayas.

Rice was the staple. Most other purchased items were nonperishable. *Iriko,* a minnow-sized dried fish, was a popular source of protein, as was *tara,* or dried codfish. To stretch the food, *iriko* was cooked with vegetables, pumpkin leaves, or chayote shoots. Codfish was broiled or cooked with soy sauce and sugar. Vegetables were homegrown and shared with friends and neighbors. Farmwives pickled cabbages, eggplant, and cucumbers to make them last.

When they were not busy with the harvest, many farmers went shore fishing. "We fried fish," Teruo Yoshida said in his autobiography, *Mongoose Hekka.* "When fried, fish lasts for days."[5]

Downwind from the home was the *benjo,* or outhouse, which was stocked with newspapers and old catalogs. The closest thing to real

A girl relaxes by the *kuriba,* or processing area, on a coffee farm, circa 1947. The round structure above is a fermentation vat. *(Gerald Kinro collection.)*

toilet paper was the soft paper that wrapped store-bought apples and oranges.[6]

For those who wet-processed coffee, additional features were necessary: the coffee pulping area, or *kuriba;* the drying platform, or *hoshidana;* and a place to store the parchment coffee.

A Culture of Hard Work

Coffee farming was especially taxing during the harvest season, which began in August and ended in early February. Because of the pressures to get the crop harvested before it fell to the ground and became useless, farmers and pickers rose before dawn and remained in the fields until after dusk—a routine they

Nothing was wasted. This old lumber stands ready for recycling into another construction project. The shed in the background is the *kuriba,* or processing area. *(Circa 1940s photo from the Hatsue Kinro collection.)*

endured every day of the week until the last coffee berry was picked.

The harvesting procedure was laborious. The fundamental tool for picking coffee was a basket made of mesh wire or woven *lauhala*, or *Pandanus* leaves. These baskets were strapped to pickers' waists or hung from their necks. When full of coffee, this basket weighed about twenty-five pounds. The picker waddled about the field trying to fill the basket as quickly as possible. The reward was emptying the basket's contents into a burlap bag and starting anew with a lighter load.

To help with picking high areas, pickers carried wooden ladders, which added another fifteen pounds or more (if they were *double*

Baskets were woven from *lauhala* for coffee harvesting. *(Photograph by Gerald Kinro, 2001.)*

At one time, coffee trees were allowed to grow tall, and harvesting required the use of a ladder. *(Kona Historical Society. Photograph by Kent Kobayashi, 1934.)*

ladders with two sets of rungs) to their burden. Harvesters carried hooks fashioned from guava or coffee sticks. They used these tools to pull inaccessible branches within reach. The hooks ended in wire loops that the harvesters could hold with their feet, keeping the branches at the desired level while freeing their hands for continued picking.

Like infantry soldiers burdened with gear, pickers assaulted the terrain and scaled the ladders. The factors that made the area so suitable for coffee now became formidable obstacles. The slopes were difficult to climb and were hazardous upon which to set ladders. When rain made the ground muddy, pickers could slip on the smooth wooden rungs. A pull on a wet branch would bring an unwelcome cold shower.

There were also bees, centipedes, and other stinging insects. There was no time to cry or to baby a sting, however. The crop had to be picked. When harvesters encountered a wasp's nest, the solution was to crumple newspaper and tie it to the end of the stick, forming a crude torch. Then it was back to picking, risking stings from angry, homeless wasps.

When the day's harvesting was done, the work was not. The picked coffee had to be hauled from the fields and to the roadside for pickup by a miller. Up until the late 1940s hauling was usually done by donkey, the famed *Kona nightingale.* Those who opted to do their own wet processing had to pulp their coffee, which required another hour or so of work, lifting bags and emptying them into the *jogo,* or funnel, that fed into the pulper.

In the early 1900s, pulping meant manually cranking a flywheel to keep the engine in motion. A single cylinder gasoline engine introduced in the 1920s made the job easier. After World War II, electric motors became common.

Only after pulping was the work finally done; then the farmer could relax in his *furo,* have dinner, and rest. He would awaken the next day for another round in the fields. For the wet processor, the routine required rising two hours earlier to wash the coffee and

spread the beans on the *hoshidana* for drying. One schooled in er-
gonomics would have looked with disdain at the process of washing and spreading. The pulped coffee sat in a knee-deep wooden
vat as bacteria did their job fermenting the slimy covering on the
coffee bean. Washing meant donning a pair of shorts and stepping
into the smelly water that made every exposed nick, scratch, and
insect bite sting.

"We washed with our feet," Yosoto Egami, an employee of the
University of Hawai'i's experiment station in Kona, told an interviewer

A hand pulper used to process coffee in the early 1900s. Photo taken at the Kona
Historical Society's Living History Farm. *(Photograph by Gerald Kinro, 2001.)*

A one-cylinder gasoline engine was used to turn the coffee pulper, replacing the hand-operated model. Photo taken at the Kona Historical Society's Living History Farm. *(Photograph by Gerald Kinro, 2001.)*

with the University of Hawai'i Oral History Project.[7] The washer often suffered back pains from churning the coffee in the rancid water with his leg to further cleanse the bean. When done with the mixing, after ten minutes or so, the work entailed bending at the waist to remove the useless *floating coffee*, coffee of low-density and, therefore, poor quality. The beans that float were skimmed off the surface during washing. Then the process required more bending, this time to scoop the good beans from the bottom of the vat and then deposit them on a screened surface to drain the

Wooden implements used for scooping washed coffee from the fermentation vat. Note that the use of these scoops required heavy bending and lifting. *(Photograph by Gerald Kinro, 2001.)*

excess water. At a furious pace, this took another twenty minutes, further aggravating an already aching back. Then the beans had to be transferred to a drying surface.

Before the 1920s farmers dried the beans on burlap bags. Several times per day they *raked* the coffee with a handcrafted wooden rake to ensure uniform drying.[8] If it rained, the drying coffee would be covered with roofing iron. The burlap bags evolved to the *hoshidana*, a wooden platform about twenty feet wide and forty feet long. Along its width were tracks made of metal pipe. Upon the tracks was an A-frame roof with metal wheels. Every morning the *hoshidana* would be pushed open to bare the drying coffee to the sun. Each evening (or when it threatened to rain) it would be pushed closed.

Parchment coffee drying on the ground in front of the Wall Hotel, circa early 1900s, Kainaliu, North Kona. *(Bishop Museum.)*

After World War II, electricity brought the *shaker*, a long, narrow conveyer system with a screen bottom that removed the excess water and transported the beans to the *hoshidana*. Still, the farmer had to take the washed coffee beans deposited by the shaker and spread them over the platform. A common way of doing this was by shoveling coffee onto a burlap bag, dragging it while walking backward to the desired spot on the platform, then dumping the load. Then all the mini-piles would be raked and spread for drying. The dried parchment coffee was then bagged and assembled for pickup by the miller.

When the pressures of harvesting were over, there was still work to be done. Branches had to be pruned with a handsaw. Some

A *hoshidana,* or drying platform, constructed without a roof during a transitional phase in coffee operations. Circa 1920s, Kahaluʻu. *(Hatsue Kinro collection.)*

branches were thick enough to require minutes of rest by the pruner before the cut was completed. Pruned branches had to be cut into smaller pieces with a sickle or machete and dragged and stacked away from foot traffic for use as firewood. Pruning took about a month.

Then it was time to fertilize the fields. This meant hauling 100-pound bags by hand, donkey, or (later) motor vehicle to various parts of the field, filling a coffee basket with caustic granules and lumbering throughout the field to nourish the trees. The farmers also used organic fertilizer. The rancid coffee pulp that had been rotting in a pile all harvesting season would be ready for the fields. Applying this fertilizer meant shoveling and hauling while smelly, sour, burning juices soaked one's torso and legs. As in harvesting, the spreading of manure was done tree by tree.

There also were weeds with which to contend. In Kona's environment, they could easily surpass a farmer's height. They had to be

Parchment coffee drying on a *hoshidana*. The wooden rake is used to stir the drying parchment coffee. The A frame in the background is the movable roof on wheels. *(Photograph by Gerald Kinro, 2001.)*

knocked down to a workable height with a sickle and then attacked with a hoe. After World War II, technology brought herbicides to help the farmer. Herbicide application was done with a knapsack sprayer weighing forty pounds when full. All day for several days the coffee farmers had to lumber through the weeds carrying sprayers on their backs.

There were other chores to be done during the off-season: Baskets had to be made, homes required repairs, tools had to be sharpened, and food needed to be grown. "Never come home empty-handed," was a common saying. Everyone returned with a bundle of firewood for the *furo*, grass for the animals, or a bag of coffee.

Then all the coffee trees would be covered with blossoms, the so-called *Kona snow*. The fragrance reminded all of the upcoming harvest season.

A Culture of Cooperation

For independent coffee farmers, working together was essential, as illustrated by the community support groups called *kumiai* or *kumi* that farmers formed according to geographic neighborhoods. Members helped each other at funerals, weddings, and in building and repairing homes. There were typically fifteen to twenty-five households in a *kumi*. In 1935 there were fifty such groups in the Kona coffee country. In 1995 there were forty-three.[9]

To appreciate the use of these groups one must know what a modern-day funeral parlor does: notifying the media, transporting family members, feeding guests, etc. The *kumi* performed these tasks on their own. When someone in the group passed away, the

Members of the Kahaluʻu *kumiai* boarding a truck for an outing circa 1950, Kahaluʻu, Kona. *(Gerald Kinro collection.)*

kumi mobilized like a well-honed military reserve unit. In the absence of telephones and the Internet, a member would go house to house to notify other members of the death. Family members then reported to a designated place. While the men made the logistical decisions, the women prepared food for all.

It seemed as though everyone knew his or her role—notification of other family members, placing announcements in the media, arranging for a minister or for burial at the cemetery—and carried it out without orders or guidance. Some waited all day at the airport for

A farmer leads a loaded donkey through a coffee field in 1934. The *Kona nightingale* was an essential part of the coffee industry until shortly after World War II. *(Kona Historical Society. Photograph by Kent Kobayashi.)*

After World War II, Jeeps replaced donkeys on Kona's coffee farms. *(University of Hawai'i Oral History Project, courtesy of the Reverend Shugen Komagata.)*

family members arriving from off-island. When there were no hearses, a member of the group transported the casket in his vehicle. Thus, the grieving family was spared much of the labor and pain of planning the funeral.

The *kumi* mobilized the same way for other projects. When building needed to be done, the members typically avoided hiring a contractor. Instead a carpenter was hired to lead the project, and the members, with their own tools, followed.[10]

The *kenjin-kai,* or prefectural organizations, were made of people who came from the same prefecture in Japan. These groups played a less prominent role than the *kumi.* There was only one *kenjin-kai,* made up of Kumamoto Prefecture immigrants, in Kona.

This group was close-knit because those from the same prefecture exhibited a certain pride in their origins. The Kumamoto Kenjin-Kai had three offices with seventy families in the late 1930s.[11]

Under the leadership of physician Harvey Saburo Hayashi, farmers organized their own Japanese language schools to teach their children the language and prepare them for the return to the homeland.[12] The first such school was built in 1898 in Hōlualoa. To

Kona coffee farmers created their own entertainment. Community members formed the cast of this play, which raised funds for the Hōlualoa Japanese Language School. Circa 1920s, Hōlualoa, Kona. *(Hatsue Kinro collection.)*

Members of the all-male cast of a *shibai,* or play, stand in front of a water tank. These tanks were the source of water for homes, schools, and other public places for a significant part of the twentieth century. Circa 1920s. *(Hatsue Kinro collection.)*

fund the endeavor, farmers put on *shibai,* or plays, and charged admission. Language schools were popular, with virtually every child attending until the sixth grade. The schools were closed during World War II but reopened after the war, as *Nisei,* the second generation of Japanese Americans, were eager to have their children learn Japanese.[13] The number of schools gradually declined, however, and by 2000 the school in Kealakekua was the only one remaining.

Another leader who made major contributions was the physician Yoshio Sugamura.[14] Sugamura helped the Kona farmers form their own hospital, the Kona Japanese Hospital, in 1929 in response to discrimination at the Kona County Hospital. The hospital remained open until World War II and then closed along with other institutions that were Japanese.

The Role of Women

When speaking of Kona coffee farmers, *work* and *struggle* are unisex terms because women did virtually everything that the men did except heavy lifting. Instead of lifting a whole bag of coffee, they would empty a full bag into many smaller containers to tote. They helped harvest, prune, fertilize, and clear the land. Kame Okano recalled spending hours in the hot sun next to her husband, clearing the land with a hoe. When not pregnant, she harvested coffee, pruned trees, and applied fertilizer.[15]

Women also did the household chores, such as cooking and cleaning. During the off-season they wove new coffee baskets for the next harvest season out of *lauhala,* the leaves of the *Pandanus* plant. They also wove hats, purses, and so forth to sell in order to augment the family income. Women tended vegetable gardens and helped feed the hogs that they kept. Popular foods such as pickled vegetables and *natto,* fermented soy beans, were made at home by the women. Women constructed raincoats and crafted footwear with soles made of old tire rubber.

Because of the double burden of farm- and housework, it could be argued that the women worked harder than the men did.

The Role of Children

The boy charged to bring the bags of harvested coffee from the fields was about 11 or 12 years old. He secured those bags, which weighed more than 100 pounds apiece, and loaded three of them onto the donkey. The steep, muddy terrain of Hualālai was too much for even the most sure-footed of beasts. The ground shifted, and the donkey slipped and fell. With the animal on the ground, the boy unloaded the bags, got the donkey up, and reloaded to take another chance on the slopes. This scenario was not uncommon. "I know, many times, I used to cry," recalled Minoru Inaba.[16]

Children joined in the farmwork, laboring alongside their parents by their late preteen years. Many started by picking up ripe coffee that fell to the ground. When the children entered school, they typically were awarded their first picking baskets and were charged with picking the low branches of a tree. Gradually, hooks and ladders were added to a child's harvesting arsenal. Other chores included caring for younger siblings while the parents worked, starting fires for heating the *furo*, housecleaning, cooking, and cleaning the outhouse. During the off-season, they tended the vegetable gardens and fed the hogs.

So important were children's contributions to farmwork that in 1932 the local schools adopted the coffee school schedule, which made the school year last from November to August and moved vacation to coincide with the coffee harvest. A survey done by C.J. Griswold, the principal of Konawaena Elementary and High School, showed the following numbers of bags of coffee picked by his students per year:

1932: 25,320
1933: 21,660
1934: 34,579
1935: 23,641
1936: 41,821
1937: 50,737[17]

Griswold also estimated that another 15,000 bags of coffee were picked by grammar school students from the other schools in Kona. He concluded that Kona's students picked 65,737 bags of coffee and collectively saved their parents $31,500 in harvesting costs in 1937.[18] (Pickers were paid by the number of bags harvested, and Griswold must have used 50 cents per bag as the basis for his calculations.)

These figures represent about 16 percent of the coffee harvested in 1937 if we assume that the total amount of coffee harvested in Kona was about 400,000 bags—a reasonable estimate based on production data for that period.[19] Furthermore, Griswold estimated that his students worked 82,000 hours performing other farmwork in 1937. At 15 cents an hour, they performed the equivalent of $12,300 of work. By adding this figure to the amount of money they saved by assisting with the harvest, it can be shown that they saved their parents a total of about $44,000.[20]

From 1932 to 1937 the University of Hawai'i Cooperative Extension Service estimated annual gross receipts from coffee to be $167 per acre. Expenditures, not including family labor, were $96 per acre, for a net profit of $76 per acre.[21] With about 5,000 acres of coffee,[22] children saved their parents nearly $9 per acre.

Although the statistical validity of Griswold's research methodology is not known, the figures are plausible because it was customary for families to have many children who did farmwork. Some families had no children above age 7 at the time of the survey. Some had many, and these families benefited the most from child labor. Edwin Kaneko, who grew up in Keauhou, North Kona, during those years, recalled starting to pick coffee and doing other farmwork at about age 4 or 5. "By twelve, our work outputs equaled an adult's," he said.[23] Like other children, he was taught to never come home empty-handed. There was always a bag of coffee or a load of firewood to transport. There were always chores to be done. Only when farmwork was done could children do their schoolwork.

Children were socialized in the ways of self-sufficiency, cooperation, and family responsibility as well. Teruo Yoshida told the story of the pig he had raised as a boy. He diligently cut grass for it and fed it avocados and papayas. It became a special friend to him. His financially needy family, however, was forced to sell his animal. He recalled crying as the buyer loaded the pig onto the truck to take it away, knowing the pig was destined to end up as food. When later asked why he never tried to stop the sale, he replied: "You don't question your parents."[24]

When children wanted toys, they made their own. Yoshida described a pocketknife as a boy's best friend.[25] "When we needed a fishing pole, we cut one. We made our own slingshots with a branch from a guava tree and rubber from a cast-off inner tube," Edwin Kaneko said.[26] Children were gradually brought into the *kumi* culture by living in it. They attended social events and watched their parents at work. They helped by doing small chores. All through this, a bond with neighbors was being forged. When they were old enough, the children joined their parents in working for the mutual good.

There were organizations such as baseball teams and the Boy Scouts. For the most part, however, children's activities revolved around the school. This is where they saw their friends. Other forms of entertainment were plays and movies that periodically traveled to Kona. Minoru Inaba, born in 1904, recalls seeing movies as a youngster; electricity for the traveling show was provided by a generator.[27]

Parents stressed the importance of education to their children. There was, however, no high school in Kona until 1921. Students such as Masaji Marumoto, the first Asian American to graduate from Harvard Law School and later a Hawai'i State Supreme Court Justice, had to go to Honolulu.

In 1921, five students came together to form the first graduating class of Konawaena High School, the class of 1925.[28] Among them was Inaba, who would return to Konawaena as a teacher and administrator and, later, would serve as a legislator. After finishing grade school in Hōlualoa, Inaba worked for a year until the high school opened its doors. He recalled playing sports for the school, especially football. The team had no coach; instead the players ordered books and magazines and made their own plays.[29] Inaba recalled getting "dirty lickings" when his team played Hilo High.[30]

Despite the emphasis on education, many children did not finish high school prior to World War II. Their labor was too critical to the family's survival. The oldest children were often required to sacrifice

In its early years, Konawaena High School's football team played without a coach. Photo circa early 1920s, Kealakekua, Kona. *(Hatsue Kinro collection.)*

their education for the benefit of the younger children, leaving school to work on the farm or elsewhere to help support the family.[31]

Major Changes

By the end of World War II, most of the farmers were of the second generation. They began installing electricity and other conveniences, such as kerosene stoves, modern lighting, appliances, and telephones. Municipal water came to Kona in the 1960s, and farmers gradually became reliant on the system.

Some coffeehouses still remained until the turn of the century, however, along with their water tanks, gardens, pig pens, fruit trees, and outhouses.

The *kumi* remained strong going into the twenty-first century. Although originally Japanese, these organizations became multiethnic. Other organizations to help farmers arose, such as the Farm Bureau and the Kona Coffee Council. Despite the changes, however, coffee farming remained difficult, demanding independence, toughness, co-operation, and self-sufficiency. How did the farmers survive their hardships? "We just had to," Howard Tatsuno said.[32]

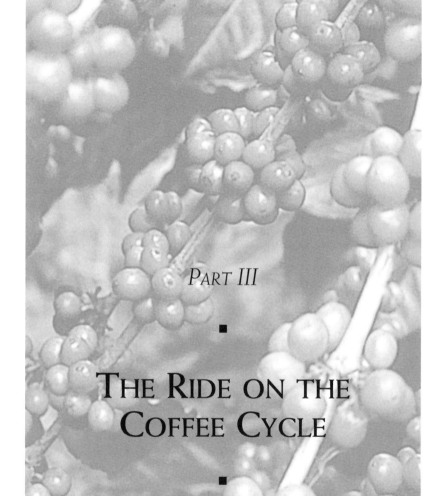

PART III

THE RIDE ON THE
COFFEE CYCLE

CHAPTER 5

ROCK BOTTOM ROAD
THE DARK YEARS

The Coffee Cycle

Historically, coffee has been a "boom and bust" crop. The old law of supply and demand is further affected by growth lags and coffee's *alternate-bearing* nature—coffee normally produces a poor crop after a good one.[1]

Yields peak around 15 to 20 years after planting a new tree. Coffee plants exhaust their harvest potential and are uprooted and then replaced. During periods of high prices, growers all over the world are encouraged to plant more coffee and to switch to coffee from other crops. Some clear new lands to plant more. Because of a three-year lag from planting to harvest, prices have usually dropped before the new plantings produce. The new plantings all come to fruition when prices are low. This gluts the market, further lowering prices.[2] Furthermore, periods of high prices last only for a few years, while low prices continue much longer. In 1906 Brazil began the practice of withholding coffee from the market to create huge stockpiles. They released these reserves when their production was low and prices were high. This attempt to control prices is called *valorization*.

The Coffee Cycle and Hawai'i

In coffee's history of ups and downs, the boom in the mid-1890s expanded the industry in Hawai'i. In a sudden turn of events, the bust of 1899 caused investors to shift their interests elsewhere. This shift allowed former plantation workers to become independent coffee farmers, as larger growers in Kona gave up their holdings. In 1926, the Kona Development Company closed all of its sugar operations, making room for more coffee cultivation. From 1925 to 1930, 800 new coffee acres were added.[3] Thus the pioneers came to Kona during the bust period that lasted for about another 20 years.

World War I helped start a boom period for Kona coffee by creating a demand and bolstering prices. Another factor that helped prices was a frost in 1918 that destroyed the coffee crop in Brazil.[4] This caused a major shortage and gave coffee prices an additional boost. Kona coffee farmers entered the Roaring Twenties on a high note.

This prosperity brought new farmers and pickers into Kona—more people who wanted independence and a chance at making money. Farmers such as Alvado and pickers such as Dinson were just part of the influx of people who immigrated to Kona.

Coffee prices rose to 28 cents per pound, and Kona was considered the most prosperous district in Hawai'i. A one-acre lease holding sold for $1,000, and its exports totaled $1,938,595.[5] With this prosperity, farmers borrowed money to improve their farms.[6] They installed wet-processing facilities and new structures. They looked toward the future with optimism because the American dream they had toiled for seemed to be within reach.

Then as sharply as the prices rose in 1918, the stock market crash of 1929 sent coffee prices spiraling downward. Farmers, prosperous a year before, found themselves deep in debt with only low-priced coffee to sustain them.

There were other problems that persisted. Rats were still attacking coffee, and so the coffee farmers hunkered down and raised

$3,000 from community donations to form a rat-eradication program that paid local children for each rat tail they collected.

The economy continued its downward spiral. With the price of coffee low, pickers explored other options. Dinson traded in his basket for a jump rope and boxing gloves to earn money as a prizefighter. After a few fights, however, Dinson ended his boxing career. He and his new bride left Kona for the Hāmākua Coast, where he resumed work on a sugar plantation.[7]

Like Dinson, Santana saw his earnings drop from $1 a bag to 50 cents a bag, then 40 cents a bag, and then 25 cents a bag. Loving the independence Kona afforded, however, he opted to stay. He lived simply, paying rent of $1.50 per month. He took jobs clearing coffee fields with a hoe for 35 cents per day, which was divided among five people. Santana also took on jobs building stone walls for landowners, doing construction for the Work Progress Administration, and clearing land for a rancher. Santana called his barehanded work clearing lots "pulling guava."[8]

With pickers choosing other work, there was a lack of harvesters. Partly because of this shortage, the Kona coffee school schedule was inaugurated in 1932.[9]

The low prices put farmers, already struggling, even deeper in debt. Farmers saw their unlimited annual credit accounts with the stores halted and replaced by a maximum of $5 per acre per month. As prices dropped even lower, farmers saw this credit allowance shrink to $3 per acre per month to $2.50 per acre per month.[10]

Ariyoshi, a college student in Honolulu, called Kona coffee "feeble." As a son of a coffee farmer, he was highly critical of the credit system in which the farmers were caught. He recalled his days as a store clerk. A farmer cried and pleaded with him for more food, as his $20 food allowance per month was not enough for him, his wife, and their eight children. Sacrificing his share of food for the children, the farmer ate crackers soaked in water.[11] Ariyoshi said that another weakness of the credit system was the unwillingness of grocers to advance items unless farms were well maintained, yet it was the poorer farmers who had difficulty maintaining their farms.[12]

Also affected was the farmers' ability to borrow money. Many farmers mortgaged their farms to remain in production, and they needed money to pay off the mortgages. Most farmers needed loans to operate. The only banks in Kona were the Bank of Hawai'i and the Bishop Bank (later renamed First Hawaiian Bank). Neither would extend credit to the Kona farmers. By 1935 some had debts so large that they gave up and fled with their hopes of wealth and independence crushed. Others went bankrupt. From 1929 to 1938, the number of farms dropped from 1,070 to 600. The number of acres in coffee decreased from 5,498 in 1929 to 4,372 in 1938.[13] Of the remaining farms, most were mortgaged for six to 30 years. Kona coffee faced extinction.

One of the many people credited with keeping the industry alive is Julian Yates, a member of the County of Hawai'i Board of Supervisors. Yates initiated and kept public works projects in Kona so farmers could earn needed cash. Many used this cash to hire laborers to maintain their farms. Others used it to survive.[14]

Credit Where Credit Is Due

Earl Nishimura, a county agricultural extension agent with the University of Hawai'i, organized the Kona Advancement Club for the second generation of farmers. Here, the *Nisei* spoke of ways to obtain credit, improve their farms and their crops, and make Kona a better place. They organized coffee schools where farmers could learn more about the commodity they were growing and about the latest scientific methods.[15]

A young farmer inspired by these schools was Haruyoshi Akamatsu. Akamatsu went further and explored the subject of credit by cochairing, with Albert Shimizu, a study group sponsored by the Central Kona Young Men's Association. He was determined to find ways in which farmers could help themselves. His group wrote letters to government agencies and mainland universities to see how other farm communities coped with financial problems. Through his correspondence Akamatsu learned how credit unions had been successful in Europe a century earlier. The U.S. Congress had given credit unions legal status; they were tax-exempt and regulated and insured by an agency of the federal government. He and his committee found the concept of the credit union—the self-ownership of a financial institution—most appealing.

The Central Kona Young Men's Association invited representatives from other Kona associations to hear a speaker from the mainland explain the mechanics of a credit union. On a stormy night, they met. Among the leaders present were Peter Hirata, of Hōnaunau; Yosoto Egami, of Kainaliu; Albert Shimizu, of Central Kona; Satoru Omoto, of Kealakekua; and Yoshiichi Ujimori, of

Haruyoshi Akamatsu led Kona's credit union movement. *(Fujiko Akamatsu collection, courtesy of Samuel Camp.)*

Honalo.[16] Akamatsu and the guest speaker persuaded the others that the credit union was the best for them. They wished to start immediately, but there were not enough people at the meeting to organize a credit union. Determined to launch a credit union, Akamatsu and his colleagues went house-to-house in the rain to get enough signatures for the charter. In an all-night effort, they obtained forty-three signatures, then rousted an attorney out of bed early in the morning to notarize the documents. The Kona Farmers' Credit Union was born in 1936. Members elected Hirata as board chairman, a position he held for more than 20 years in addition to his duties as a farmer and educator. The credit union's first manager was William Ishida.[17]

The early years were difficult for the new institution. Although the membership fee was just 25 cents, shares were $5, an exorbitant amount for many during those times. Therefore, although many members wished to borrow money, assets were low because of the small membership base. Acting on a recommendation of Yates, the credit union expanded the opportunity for membership to all residents of Kona.[18] In 1939, the institution became the Kona Community Federal Credit Union. It was Yates who gave his time and energy to promote the credit union to all. The increased membership brought additional capital, and loans became available. The Kona coffee farmers were fighting back.

Despite the formation of the credit union, many farmers still owed large sums to American Factors. With coffee prices still low, prospects of the repayment of these debts and for the coffee industry were dim. Those dealing with American Factors had an estimated total of $1.1 million in debts—$895,000 to stores, $168,000 to banks, and $8,700 to individuals. The average debt for each farm was $1,777.[19] In 1938 a group of farmers met with members of American Factors in Honolulu. The leader of the farmers was Morihara, a coffee broker and storeowner.[20] Ariyoshi reported the meeting as secret and provided no other details.[21]

A store invoice showing debt adjustment by American Factors. Despite the significant amount of debt overlooked, it took five years to pay the remaining balance of $500. *(Fujiko Akamatsu collection, courtesy of Samuel Camp.)*

When results of the meeting were finally announced, American Factors agreed to forego all but 2 percent of the debt owed by farmers.[22] In addition, the legislature assisted by granting a tax exemption to farms as long as coffee prices remained less than 10 cents per pound. Through the courage and efforts of many, Kona coffee had been saved from extinction.

Diversification

Cyrus McCormack, the agriculturist who invented the combine, cautioned people not to put all their eggs in a single basket. The University of Hawai'i Cooperative Extension Service echoed this caveat. Another advocate of diversification was Yates, who felt that it was difficult for Kona to sustain itself on coffee alone and that it made good sense to have a backup industry in case of a failure, such as the one the farmers were experiencing.[23] Farmers got a boost from the government when the Farm Stabilization Administration provided loans totaling $100,000 to coffee farmers, provided they diversify their plantings.[24]

This diversification was not easy, however, because of coffee's characteristics. It takes three years for a coffee plant to mature. During this period, the grower must provide constant care to the crop. After much tending, there is an emotional attachment to the plant. The tree is expected to last for many years. Therefore, it is difficult to simply replant an area. A gradual change is usually required.

Furthermore, the farmers could diversify only with another orchard-type crop because of the hilly, rocky terrain in Kona. Most areas are not suited for vegetables, for machinery will simply not work on the volcanic slopes.

However, there were some farmers who were daring and ambitious enough to take the lead and venture into something new. In the late 1930s some Kona farmers began diversifying their farms by planting macadamia nuts.

Researcher Edward Fukunaga desuckers coffee trees pruned in the old Kona way.
(University of Hawai'i Cooperative Extension Service.)

A New Beginning?

In 1940, Nishimura, the extension agent who had started the coffee school, left Kona to pursue a career in law. His replacement was Edward Fukunaga. Fukunaga was not a stranger to Kona farmers, for he had served as an interpreter at the coffee school and even instructed at some of the sessions.[25]

Fukunaga, who assumed the position in 1941, planned to stay in Kona for five years and then move on. His career as an agent was shortened, however. With the start of World War II, he volunteered for military service.[26] The importance of his brief tenure of a few months was not what he taught the farmers but the mark that Kona left on him. He would return after the war, this time as an agricultural research scientist. Under his leadership, Kona would become a world leader in coffee research.

The stage was set for something big. *Nisei* had begun taking over their parents' farms. They started to diversify their crops, and their new credit union was growing. Debts to American Factors had all but been erased, and a new beginning loomed, even with low prices. No one, however, could predict what happened 170 miles away on December 7, 1941. The farmers found their country at war.

CHAPTER 6

THE WORLD WAR II YEARS

After the bombing of Pearl Harbor, Kona schools closed for several months. When students of Hōlualoa School returned, they found that the army had taken over their campus. Hawai'i was a staging area for the war in the Pacific, and the school quartered the soldiers. Teachers and students made do in empty buildings in this little North Kona village. Eventually, after the army found more suitable facilities elsewhere in the community, the teachers and students went back to their school. Students participated in gas mask drills, air raid drills, and food stocking drives. Classes were often disrupted by the sound of convoys and troops conducting maneuvers in nearby fields.[1] This arrival of troops was a boon to those businesses that catered to soldiers. Restaurants, stores, and bars in Kona thrived.

Under martial law, Hawai'i was put under the control of a military governor. Blackouts were mandated from 7:45 p.m. to 6:15 a.m., severely restricting the farmers' work. Furthermore, the military government divided Kona into North Kona and South Kona, and travel between the two districts was restricted. This was a sharp contrast with the free passage residents had enjoyed in the past. Beaches became off-limits and deep sea fishing was prohibited.

Many Japanese found their homes searched and their property confiscated. *Issei* (first-generation Japanese in America) community and business leaders, language school teachers, and Buddhist ministers were arrested and incarcerated. Among them were Morihara and Akamatsu. Morihara owned the Morihara Store and the Sun Mellow Coffee Company. He had played a huge part in the debt-adjustment negotiations with American Factors. He would spend four years in an internment camp, forcing the closure of his coffee brokerage business. Because of his efforts to help the farmers, the government suspected him "of being a radical."[2] Akamatsu was the force behind the credit union's birth. He happened to be on the mainland United States when internment began. After his release, he settled in Arizona.[3]

The home of Kazo Tanima was searched three times before authorities were satisfied that he was not a threat. According to Tanima, Japanese were followed whenever they went shopping or for walks. Watchmen were placed outside the homes of all Japanese residents of Hōlualoa.[4]

As in other American communities, the effort in Kona was to win the war. Men left to enter the military, causing a labor shortage on coffee farms. An arrangement to recruit ninety-four high school students from other parts of the island helped save the crop in 1942. These young harvesters were placed in a recreational camp erected at Konawaena School.[5]

In spite of the hardships, the war played a big part in improving coffee prices. The army purchased the entire Kona coffee crop. Subsequently, Hawai'i's military governor increased the price of parchment coffee by 3/4 cents per pound, citing high labor costs and low ceiling prices as pressing issues.[6]

The gradual increase of coffee prices made life easier, but farmers still survived as they had in the past—by saving and living off the land. Many housewives turned to weaving *lauhala* goods to help with the family income. By the war's end, 85 percent of all *lauhala* goods sold in the territory were from Kona. Of these, 75 percent came from Japanese households, most of them the households of coffee farmers.[7]

In their own independent way, Kona coffee farmers maintained stability and lived out the war years.

CHAPTER 7

TALES OF VERTICALS

Vertical Movement

By the end of World War II, most of the coffee farmers were of the second generation and were seeking to improve what their parents had started. The farms were evolving as Jeeps replaced donkeys as the new beasts of burden. Many of the second-generation farmers had to persuade their parents that modernization was the way to go, for the thought of turning over productive land for a Jeep trail was distasteful. Many began installing electricity to process their coffee and to power their homes. Many of them purchased appliances. With prices for coffee higher, the farmers looked to the future with anticipation.

The post-war years also saw some new farmers. Among them was Dinson, the picker/boxer who left Kona during the Great Depression. Dinson returned to set up his own farm in Hōnaunau, South Kona. He would later sell his farm and open a pool hall. Nevertheless, he was eager to be his own boss when he started.[1] Joining him as a new farmer was Santana, the picker who survived the Great Depression by clearing land with his bare hands. Santana purchased a farm in Kahaluʻu, North Kona.[2] Despite having his own farm, he and his family continued to work as pickers, helping other families in the neighborhood.

Parchment coffee prices dipped to an all-time low of 17.8 cents per pound in 1946[3] before rising to a high of 28 cents per pound in 1949.[4] Despite rising prices, however, the yield from Kona was small, a mere 50 to 75 percent of the area's normal output.[5] The farmers continued their defensive mode. Reports confirmed that Kona, still largely dependent on coffee, was not doing well economically. A 1950 report released by the Territory of Hawai'i showed that the Kona area was depressed. This was a sharp contrast to a report released 20 years prior that had shown Kona to be the most prosperous district in Hawai'i. According to the 1950 report, the median family income in both North and South Kona was well below the median family income in both Hawai'i and Honolulu counties:

North Kona	$1,157
South Kona	$1,141
All Hawai'i County	$2,341
Honolulu County	$3,179[6]

Despite the improvements made by some farmers, half of the households in Kona had no electricity, well over half had no refrigerator, and 38 percent had no running water.[7] The fortunes of Kona's economy and of its people still followed the fate of world coffee prices, which were recovering but had not yet bounced back entirely.

The movement for diversified agriculture continued. In 1950, Hawai'i Governor Ingram Stainback signed a bill that appropriated funds to begin a water development plan for Kona. This made further agricultural development possible. In 1952 the trustees of the Bishop estate, the largest landholder in Kona, created a land control and development division. This was the initial phase of turning Kona's wastelands into productive small farms for coffee, macadamia nuts, dairies, taro, and pasture.[8]

Diversification took other forms as the tourist industry that Yates had advocated for the district was now coming to fruition with the construction of an airport and new hotels. In 1951, 18,400 tourists visited Kona. This number increased to 40,000 in 1956.[9]

Boom Times

Although coffee prices had been steadily rising since the start of World War II (despite the 1946 dip), a frost in Brazil in 1953 caused another spike in the price curve.[10] A year later, further developments in Brazil, along with bad weather, caused a worldwide coffee shortage, resulting in even higher prices. Kona coffee entered another boom period.[11]

The *Hilo Tribune Herald* reported that the future of Kona coffee was as secure as ever.[12] R.L. Hind of the Captain Cook Coffee Company spoke of expanding his coffee operations and encouraged farmers to do the same. By then, most of the original leases to farmers expired with the Captain Cook Coffee Company. It had made land more readily available and even sold parcels so its employees could live in their own homes.[13] More farmers moved toward independence in marketing, and more stores did a cash-and-carry business. This reflected a trend away from the old system in which farmers were at the mercy of the millers and their stores.

A combination of increased production and peak prices made coffee the third-leading crop in the Territory of Hawai'i behind sugar and pineapple in 1957. Coffee accounted for 5.2 percent of all crop sales.[14] A year later, despite slightly lower prices, there was a record-breaking output of almost 18,496,000 pounds of parchment coffee, which was valued at $7 million.[15] As a result of this prosperity, there were twelve coffee mills in Kona.[16]

Integrating the Verticals

A coffee plant is like a Christmas tree in one respect: It has main upright branches called *verticals*. Coming off the verticals are smaller twig-like branches called *horizontals*. It is the job of a coffee vertical to produce more horizontals. As a vertical grows taller, more horizontals appear. The job of a horizontal is to produce coffee flowers and subsequently cherries. They also produce more horizontals, which will also bear fruit and produce more horizontals.[17]

There are limits, however. First, a tree can take only so much stress and has to be pruned to prevent dieback and a decrease in production. Second, coffee bears only on the previous year's new growth. These characteristics make coffee an alternate-bearing crop, with a poor crop usually following a good one.[18]

It was Fukunaga, the county agent for a few months before World War II, who used this information and, with scientist John Beaumont, developed a pruning system that resulted in an efficient, productive coffee tree. They advocated limiting a tree to four verticals and *total renewal,* the pruning of all verticals at one time. All trees in a row were to be pruned at the same time, making all the verticals in a row the same age, not exceeding four years. The ages of the different rows varied from one to four years.

When Fukunaga and Beaumont published their proposal in 1956 it seemed radical to most Kona farmers, who were used to keeping as many as six verticals on a tree. Each year farmers pruned the oldest vertical from the tree, leaving five or more and allowing a new vertical to form in place of the one just removed. Instead of just one forming, however, several sprouted, and the grower had to choose the best vertical and manually remove the extraneous ones, a process called *me-kagi,* or desuckering. Trees pruned in the traditional manner grew to a height of up to twenty feet, making harvesting difficult and necessitating the use of ladders.

The new system was easier. A farmer no longer had to look for a suitable branch to cut. When all rows in a field were adapted to this system, he could simply cut the oldest rows. Each year, three-fourths of the trees would be bearing because it takes time for a tree to begin fruiting after pruning. The new system overcame coffee's alternate-bearing characteristic and produced a more consistent crop over a longer period of time.

The new system saved labor because no longer did farmers have to spend as much time at *me-kagi*. The shorter pruning cycle resulted in smaller trees. This reduced the need to prop up older branches that became too heavy when they bore fruit. Most important, the shorter trees made harvesting easier and faster, eliminating the need for ladders. The result was less waste with fewer over-ripe cherries to fall. Coupled with timed fertilizer applications,[19] also endorsed by Fukunaga, tree efficiency was maximized. This method became known as the Beaumont-Fukunaga, or BF, system and revolutionized coffee production in Latin America. It would, however, take time to catch on in Kona.

In later years, Fukunaga would be highly regarded for his coffee research, which began in 1947 when he assumed directorship of the University of Hawai'i's experiment station in Kainaliu.[20] Kona, despite producing a mere one-tenth of 1 percent of the world's coffee, became recognized as the world's leader in coffee research. Fukunaga published no fewer than forty articles on the practical aspects of producing coffee and macadamia nuts. His work would not only improve Kona coffee but could possibly be credited with saving it.

Vertical Integration—The First Steps

The idea of forming a cooperative in which the farmers controlled markets was appealing to many. In 1955, the first cooperative, the Kona Coffee Cooperative (KCC), was organized. Its processing facilities were headquartered in Kahalu'u, North Kona, the famed "Donkey Mill." Its manager was George Harada.

That same year Noguchi, the owner of his own mill, filed papers to have his company become a cooperative.[21] You have to see what the enemy is doing, and then keep up, he told an interviewer.[22] He could see the desire of farmers to try another venue of marketing, and he feared that many of his farmers would leave and join KCC if he did not act. He called his cooperative the Pacific Coffee Cooperative (PCC). Other mills followed. Despite these cooperatives, however, there was little standard in uniformity in the products they delivered. They had very little organization.

The man credited with revolutionizing the marketing of Kona coffee at that time is Takeshi Kudo,[23] a second-generation farmer. Kudo's father, Takumi, began farming in South Kona in the 1920s. Takumi Kudo eventually became a coffee broker and sold green coffee to mainland companies.

With his five brothers and sister the young Takeshi Kudo worked the farm and experienced firsthand the difficulties of farming. The hard work and other difficulties of farming did not deter him, however. On the contrary, Kudo loved agriculture. He left during World War II to serve with the 442nd Regimental Combat Team. Upon his return to Kona after the war, he began working the fields while other veterans sought "better" occupations. Kudo was bright and was a natural farmer. He introduced innovative concepts to his operation, such as mulching and new herbicide application methods. He continued learning all he could about the art and science of farming.

His farm stood out among the rest. For his efforts, he was chosen as the territory's outstanding young farmer of 1956 and sent to Durham, North Carolina, to compete with other contestants from across the United States. Kudo was selected as a finalist for the big prize.[24]

This trip was one of the turning points for Kona coffee, not because of the awards Kudo received but because of the knowledge he gained. After the competition, Kudo toured the southern farm belt. He was impressed with the cooperatives organized and owned by the farmers there. He saw the advantages the cooperatives gave their members by supplying them with farm supplies at lower than market cost. He thought that such organization would benefit Kona farmers.

Upon his return from the mainland, he and his father started the Sunset Coffee Cooperative with twenty-seven members.[25] The existing co-ops were able to serve only those who wet-processed their harvest and delivered parchment. To Kudo, this was not acceptable because it left a void for those farmers without wet-processing facilities. He organized these farmers and arranged for their coffee to be wet-processed at the facilities of the Captain Cook Coffee Company.

Takeshi Kudo of the Sunset Coffee Cooperative stands and addresses members of the Kona Coffee Association and representatives of the Hawai'i state government. Included in the photo are Mikio Izu, Masao Tanaka, Wilbert Okada, Yoshio Noguchi, Charles Cecil, and Mits Morashige. (*Kona Historical Society, photograph by Adrian Saxe 1962.*)

Kudo also observed that the other co-ops, despite including 400 of the 800 Kona coffeegrowers, were not successful because of the individualism of the growers and a lack of leadership from their officers.[26] Kudo was determined to bring about true organization, and he began planning a strategy to improve the situation of Kona coffee.

Problems Lurk

Kudo and other observers saw problems for the Kona coffee industry. Despite a superior product and technical advantages, the Kona coffee industry had little clout. Kona could not compete with the low labor costs of other parts of the world or with the power of large distributors such as General Foods. In addition, Kona coffee

was losing its identity because it was being shipped to San
Francisco, where it was blended with other national and regional
varieties. Kona produced a mere 0.1 percent of the world's coffee.
As a result, events abroad dictated the prices and other activities in
Kona. American Factors had prospered only because the prices following World War II had been high, but now the industry faced another bust. Prices peaked in 1957, and African countries, eager to
capitalize, increased production. They exported huge quantities of
the cheaper *C. canephora.* To control prices, Brazil added to their
huge stockpiles of coffee that by 1959 equaled total world ex-
ports.[27] Brazil practiced stockpiling, or *valorization,* to control
prices, in the same way OPEC does with oil. As a small producer,
Kona was dragged along for another wild ride.

The decade's end also brought an end to an era in which the
Dillingham Corporation purchased the Captain Cook Coffee
Company from the Hind family. Perhaps the biggest event of the
1950s occurred in 1959 when Hawai'i was admitted to the union.
In Kona, coffee farmers celebrated statehood with the rest of
Hawai'i because they, too, had dreamed of being equal to their
mainland counterparts. That same year, they harvested a record
5,900 acres of coffee.[28] Despite the euphoria, however, the farmers
were aware of the shaky ground on which their industry rested. The
coffee business was much like the steep, muddy slopes that sus-
tained their lives; it could shift at any time and topple even the most
sure-footed donkeys.

CHAPTER 8

COFFEE IN THE NEW STATE

On November 15, 1960, Konawaena High School's class of 1964, its first of the post-war baby boom generation, came together for the first time. Among the 150 or so freshmen were Ellison Onizuka and Sotero Agoot. Onizuka was to become America's first Asian-American astronaut; his life would end tragically in the explosion of the space shuttle Challenger. Agoot would lead the unified Kona farmer's cooperative into the twenty-first century. Onizuka, Agoot, and their classmates found their initiation to high school life delayed, however. Because of an unusually heavy demand for harvesting labor, the Department of Education granted a request from farmers to extend school vacations for another two weeks to enable all students to help with the coffee harvest. This delay demonstrated the importance children still played in the coffee industry. Like the students who began the school coffee schedule in 1932, and the ones surveyed by Principal Griswold in 1937, their harvesting labor was more than a luxury for their parents: It was crucial.

Students no longer needed to collect rat tails, however. In 1960, the Hawai'i Board of Health stepped into the rat eradication effort by making available twenty-three tons of poison-laced oats valued at $10,000.[1] The distribution of this modern means of mitigating the rat problem, however, used an old mechanism of distribution, the *kumi*. As in the early 1900s, the community support group still played a vital role for the farmer.

Also in 1960, a well had been dug, and the construction of a water main to service the residents of Kona was under way.

As citizens of a new state, the people of Kona also were able to help elect the nation's new president. They had already elected their representatives to the U.S. Congress as a condition of statehood. There were state offices to fill, too; the people of Kona elected Kudo, the farmer who had organized the Sunset Coffee Cooperative, to the Hawai'i House of Representatives.

Sunset Rises

Kudo recognized some of the problems the coffee industry faced. Coffee prices were in a bust period, and American Factors and the Captain Cook Coffee Company were contemplating terminating their coffee operations.

Kudo turned these facts to his advantage. Having negotiated for the use of Captain Cook's mill for wet processing, he arranged for the purchase of the Captain Cook Coffee Company with financing from the State of Hawai'i's farm loan program and the Bank of Hawai'i. The following year, in 1963, Kudo expanded Sunset's operations by purchasing the mill owned by American Factors for $250,000. He transferred the purchased equipment from American Factors' facility in Kailua-Kona to Sunset's headquarters in Nāpō'opo'o.[2]

In 1966, Kudo took Sunset another step toward *vertical integration* by opening a coffee-roasting plant. Sunset began promoting its Mauna Kea brand of roasted coffee. In just 10 years the Sunset Cooperative had become the standard-bearer of the industry. The cooperative had more than 600 members, representing 85 percent of all coffee growers in Kona and 60 percent of Kona's total production. In addition, Sunset operated a $250,000 business of selling farm equipment and supplies to its members at reduced rates. Sunset's net profit in 1966 was $65,000, all shared by its members.[3]

Quality Control

In 1963 "Instant Kona coffee" entered the market under the brand name Spice Club.[4] This stirred controversy among purists. *Instant* was the ultimate insult, denoting inferiority to many.

Kudo, although not necessarily an opponent of instant coffee, was an advocate of quality. He realized that despite Sunset's growth, there was a need for other cooperatives and mills to come together to form a united front and to give a quality product to the consumer. He realized that Kona produced too little of the world's coffee to make a dent in the market through quantity. Kona's impact would have to be achieved through quality, and any slip could mean disaster for the local coffee industry. A consumer survey performed in Honolulu in 1961 substantiated the belief that there were major problems with the quality of Kona coffee and in the practices traditionally employed by farmers.[5] Mills processed coffee differently and their output therefore varied in quality.

Kudo's first effort was to organize all cooperatives and mills to form the Kona Coffee Association. This was not an easy task, for millers, like farmers, were still highly independent. Under Kudo's leadership, however, the individuals came together and began working for a common cause—the promotion of Kona coffee.[6]

As a legislator, Kudo fought for a grading program for coffee. His efforts came to fruition in 1963 when the Hawai'i Department of Agriculture initiated a program to standardize what was being sold and assign grades to green coffee based on weight, moisture content, size, and impurities.[7] Although the standard would be amended in the future, Kona coffee finally could measure itself against a legal yardstick. This was another step toward improving Kona's coffee's position in the market.

A Slow Decline

Despite the rise of the Sunset Coffee Cooperative, a new grading program, and the formation of the Kona Coffee Association, the coffee industry suffered a slow decline. Prices were still low from the drop of 1959, as world markets were flooded with an excess of coffee. Kona, still heavily dependent on coffee, lagged behind the rest of Hawai'i economically. The regional median family incomes for 1960 demonstrated Kona's flagging economic fortunes:[8]

North Kona	$3,944
South Kona	$3,787
Entire Hawai'i County	$4,866
Honolulu	$6,366

The coffee industry also faced a labor shortage. Many young people left Kona for better-paying opportunities, and as the tourist industry grew, it competed with the coffee industry for the available workers. In 1966, the tourist industry in Kona drew 137,000 visitors, compared to 40,000 in 1960 and 18,400 in 1951.[9] Harvesters preferred the better-paying tourist industry to the hard work of coffee farming.

The movement to diversify continued as farmers planted macadamia, avocados, and bananas to keep their lands alive. In 1966 the number of acres of harvested coffee had dropped to 4,710, compared to 5,000 in 1960. Acres dedicated to macadamia increased from 350 to 490 acres, and acres planted with bananas rose from seventy to 265 acres. Coffee production declined from 12 million pounds to 7.7 million pounds with a corresponding drop in the crop's value.[10]

Some saw no future for coffee, saying it should not be saved. They cited the special privileges that coffee farmers were offered, such as an exclusion from the Employment Security Act that required the payment of unemployment insurance. Coffee farmers were also exempted from the minimum wage requirement and child labor laws.[11]

But those who farmed did so out of love and devotion to coffee. Some felt an obligation to sustain the industry. Walter Kunitake of Keōpū, North Kona, a third-generation *sansei*, graduated from

Konawaena High School in 1962. Like all children of farmers, he worked at various chores in the farm operation. Despite his dreams of continuing his education, he put his plans on hold for a year to help his parents, who desperately needed his labor.[12]

Many of his classmates left Kona for college or other jobs. Many who remained took jobs with the tourist industry. Although the population of Kona was growing, the increase was in nonagricultural areas.

There were other threats to the industry. The war in Vietnam was escalating, and those young men who did not volunteer to serve in the armed forces often received notices of induction. Television news programs inundated Kona's homes with pictures of helicopters and sounds of rifles, as well as the names of local casualties. The year 1968 brought nationwide upheaval with the Tet Offensive in Vietnam, the assassinations of the Reverend Martin Luther King, Jr., and Robert Kennedy, and the riots at the Democratic National Convention in Chicago.

Equally dramatic for Kona was the activation of the Hawai'i National Guard. The entire guard unit in Kona, an infantry rifle company, reported for active duty in May 1968. Many in the company were farmers and farmworkers, and many family farms were affected by the sudden loss of labor. One of those families affected was the Kunitakes. Two of Kunitake's brothers donned army uniforms, leaving the family short-handed. Kunitake, this time a recent college graduate, returned to assist his parents in the absence of his brothers.[13]

Needless to say, some of Kona's soldiers never returned from Vietnam, creating further hardships for all.

The End of the Coffee School Schedule

Already short of labor, farmers received another severe blow when, in 1969, the coffee school schedule ended after nearly 40 years.[14] A survey of students showed overwhelming support for the switch. Although children still played an important part in their parents' farming efforts, the results of the survey showed a shift in attitudes, and the population of Kona that was becoming more urban. Officials of the Sunset Cooperative were expectedly disappointed.

The coffee farmers braced for an uncertain future. In 10 years the number of coffee mills had gone from nineteen to just three—the three owned by the three surviving farm cooperatives.[15] Perhaps symbolically, Kudo was defeated in his re-election bid by Inaba, a member of Konawaena High School's first graduating class. Although Inaba's roots in coffee ran deep, he spent most of his adult life as an educator and did not directly deal with the industry as Kudo did.

If there was reason for optimism, however, it was the agreement reached between the Kona coffee industry and the Superior Tea and Coffee Company of Illinois. Superior agreed to purchase the entire crop of green coffee produced by the cooperatives.[16] This was Kona's foothold into the gourmet coffee market, the result of the work of Kudo and the rest of the Kona Coffee Association to promote the quality of Kona's coffee. Although Kona coffee was down, it clung to the hope of a new market.

CHAPTER 9

ON HEARTBREAK HILL

THE BEGINNING OF THE END OF THE *NISEI* ERA

In 1972, as the Vietnam War dragged on, Kona coffee appeared to be on its deathbed. Researchers at the University of Hawai'i's Department of Agricultural and Resource Economics doubted the industry's ability to survive.[1] Coffee prices were climbing, they reported, but the high cost of coffee production and the scarcity of labor made it uneconomical to grow the crop. The researchers identified three types of coffee farmers:[2]

.1. The full-time farmer who was the older farmer who still did his own wet processing. Many grew some of their own food to survive. Some intercropped with avocado to have a secondary source of income. Some farmed to maintain leases.

2. The part-time farmer who had an interest in farming but took on another job. He farmed to maintain his lease and to have a place for his family to live. This farmer did not process his coffee, selling cherry coffee instead.

3. The gleaner who harvested only abandoned or poorly maintained coffee. He was not interested in farming but had to maintain his lease. He, too, sold only cherry coffee.[3]

Harvesting still amounted to 73 percent of total labor input. Harvesters were hard to find, however. Other jobs paid too well for many to consider the hard labors on a coffee farm. When other costs were analyzed, the researchers calculated that coffee farmers' losses were too severe for them to remain in business.[4]

Many prominent people associated with the industry said coffee was on the verge of extinction. They felt that Kona farmers should switch to more profitable crops, such as flowers.[5] Former county supervisor and landowner Sherwood Greenwell said the eighty-six acres he leased to coffee farmers was a mere fraction of the 600 acres he had leased for coffee farming at the industry's peak. Of the current land in coffee, he predicted that fifty-one acres would be lost in five years. [6]

Norman Carlson of the Bishop estate reported that of its 2,350 acres of agricultural land, only 40 percent was devoted to growing coffee.[7] Noguchi of the Pacific Coffee Cooperative estimated he would lose 50 percent of his crop in five years. "The industry is definitely dying," said D.M. Fraser of the Dillingham Investment Corporation. "It doesn't look like much of this ever again will be planted in coffee."[8] Greenwell agreed, signing Kona coffee's death certificate: "It's sad. It has no future . . . It's *pau* (over)."[9]

The farmers would not accept defeat, however, and fought back. They employed new methods, following the recommendations of Fukunaga and pruning the coffee trees shorter for easier harvesting that required less labor. Shorter trees, although they made the harvest more efficient, which meant fewer wasted coffee cherries, did not come without a price; they also resulted in a smaller crop. In the 1950s, Kona coffee farmers produced 2,700 pounds of parchment per acre. With the switch to shorter trees, the harvest dropped to 2,000 pounds of parchment per acre.[10] But what the farmers lost in volume they more than made up for through labor savings and efficiency. Farmers also continued to diversify their crops. The Sunset Coffee Cooperative, renamed the Kona Farmers Cooperative, began marketing macadamia nuts for its members.

In 1974, the year observers declared Kona coffee dead, the industry was boosted by a dramatic increase in price to 76 cents per

Harvesters in the field. Starting in the 1970s, coffee trees were pruned shorter, eliminating the need for ladders during the harvest. *(Photograph by Gerald Kinro, 2001.)*

pound, more than double the 34.6 cents received during the 1971 to 1972 season. Superior Tea and Coffee was now purchasing the entire Kona coffee crop annually at a rate of 5 cents per pound over established world markets.[11] World prices received another push in 1975 when an unexpected frost destroyed much of Brazil's crop, and the Angolan revolution made deliveries of that country's crop impossible. Rain in Colombia, disease in Nicaragua, and an earthquake in Guatemala further hurt world production. As a result, world coffee prices increased five fold.[12] This unexpected windfall gave the Kona farmers a financial reward and a second wind—the strength to keep fighting.

Despite the higher prices and the efforts of the farmers, however, there were other problems, such as the weather and coffee's natural enemies. The latest pest, a dieback and decline of coffee trees, began creeping along Māmalahoa Highway. Scientists, including Fukunaga, were at work for a solution, but the answer would come nearly 30 years later, long after Fukunaga's passing.

All in all, while the decline of coffee continued through the 1970s (although it was deterred somewhat by higher prices), the industry competed for labor and coffee's tenders competed with the clock as they became the victims of age; the era of the second-generation farmer was nearing its end.

A New Use for an Old Concept

As the Kona farmers toiled, important events that would affect their industry took place on the other side of the globe. In 1978, in a speech to the delegates of an international coffee conference held in Montreuil, France, Eva Knutson introduced a new concept. She said that nuances between geographical areas, no matter how close to each other, produced coffee beans with different flavors. These differences affected the overall quality of the beans. Some say this speech gave rise to the term *specialty coffee*.[13]

The basic principle of specialty coffee was doing everything correctly; specialty coffee beans would always be well prepared, freshly roasted, and properly brewed.[14] Marketing coffee became like marketing wine; the location of a coffee farm, like the location of a vineyard, could make all the difference in the world to a connoisseur's trained palate. The world's coffee industry had been headed in this direction for two decades prior to Knutson's speech.[15]

Most in Kona never heard of Knutson or her speech, but they were already aware of its basic premise. They had seen television advertisements proclaim that a certain coffee was best because it was *mountain grown*. They had been told many times that their coffee was the best in the world because Kona was an ideal place to grow the crop. They had been taught to be careful during harvest and to process their coffee the correct way. Few, if any, however, thought of stressing something so common in the marketing of their crop. Although most had pride in the coffee they produced, few, if any, realized that the Kona name they had toiled so hard for would be worth so much in the new specialty coffee market. Nevertheless, this new idea was to play an important role in Kona during the next decade and into the twenty-first century.

CHAPTER 10

ON THE ROAD TO PURE KONA

Trees could be renewed by pruning, letting new verticals emerge to produce future crops. Such was not the case with the farmers. Their children continued leaving the farm for better jobs that promised a better life. Who was going to carry on?

Prospects appeared bleak, and the 1980s began like the decade before with experts predicting the end of Kona coffee. Greenwell reiterated what he had said nearly 10 years ago—that coffee was *pau.*[1]

Fukunaga felt that it made better sense to switch to more profitable crops.[2] Goto, director of the Hawai'i Agricultural Extension Service and retired vice chancellor of the East West Center, stated that despite good prices, the Kona coffee industry had not attracted American citizens. Goto wrote, ". . . Their dislike for the tedious hand harvesting of each individual coffee berry seems to be the reason for their willingness to give up the coffee industry."[3]

Noguchi, now retired head of the Pacific Coffee Cooperative, concurred succinctly in a 1980 interview, "Young guys, they don't want to work on the farm."[4] He gave Kona coffee five more years. The extinction of Kona's coffee industry was just a matter of time, many observers agreed.

Renewal

Despite the decline of Kona coffee in the 1960s and 1970s, Kona coffee farms had enjoyed a 554 percent increase in prices due to another frost in Brazil and sales to the gourmet coffee market.[5] By 1982, Douwe Egberts-Superior (formerly Superior Tea and Coffee) was purchasing 70 percent of Kona's coffee output and paying an unprecedented $2.90 per pound for green Kona coffee.[6]

In a further boost to prices, United Coffee, another gourmet coffee company, was ready to compete and purchase Kona coffee at premium prices. Because of inadequate supply, however, Kona coffee was still blended with coffees from other parts of the world, and the product could not be marketed as pure Kona.[7]

During this period of good prices, new farmers saw potential in the specialty coffee market and began to grow Kona coffee. The *Nisei* were retiring, but contrary to the dire predictions of experts such as Greenwell and Noguchi there were younger people eager to farm coffee. In the 1980s and 1990s, Kona saw an influx of new farmers. Some were third generation, the children and grandchildren of coffee farmers. Some were newcomers.

For Kunitake of Keōpū, North Kona, it was as though he had never left. He had helped his parents after graduation from high school and after college. Clinging to his dreams of an education, he continued in graduate school at the University of Hawai'i, where he earned his master's degree, and at the University of Arkansas, where he earned his doctoral degree. Kunitake had always returned to help on the farm during his vacations.[8]

A certified public accountant, Kunitake taught accounting at the University of Hawai'i and at Pennsylvania State University. He returned to Kona to become director of the University of Hawai'i's West Hawai'i campus in Kealakekua, South Kona. He began farming part-time while working for the university. After studying his own situation and that of Kona coffee, he made his move into full-time coffee growing, processing, and roasting.[9]

A few miles down the road in Hōlualoa, Kunitake's cousin Jon Kunitake took over the family farm after a successful career as a jockey. Like the Kunitakes, Lee Sugai of Keauhou, North Kona, came from a family of coffee farmers. Sugai gave up a promising career as an aeronautical engineer and returned to the farm, also going into milling and roasting. These three were among several who heard Kona calling and came home to the farm.

Bob and Cea Smith were born with sugar in their blood, the progeny of sugar plantation managers. Bob Smith had planned on a career in sugar. He studied tropical crop production at the University of Hawai'i and took his diploma to C. Brewer and Company, a major sugar producer in Hawai'i. During his tenure with the company, which took him to Maui and Hilo, he rose to crop control superintendent.[10]

During the early 1980s, however, he could see that the future of sugar in Hawai'i was not good. He also yearned for the independence of operating his own farm. After much searching, he found available land in Hōnaunau, South Kona.[11] Like his predecessors 100 years ago, he desired to leave the plantation for greater independence, and Kona gave him that opportunity.

Some familiar *kama'aina* (local) surnames joined Smith. Long-time Kona residents Norman Greenwell and his son Tom began their coffee farm in 1985 in Kealakekua, South Kona.[12] They were descendents of H.N. Greenwell, the nineteenth-century coffee exporter. Desmond and Lisen Twigg-Smith began operations in Kahalu'u, North Kona, while cousin Christian Twigg-Smith hung hooks in nearby Hōlualoa.

Many newcomers moved to Kona coffee country from the mainland. John and Vicki Swift independently moved to Kona in the early 1970s to seek a different lifestyle. There they met and married. John Swift worked as a firefighter, and Vicki Swift held different jobs. She wanted the independence of working on her own. Like her predecessors who moved to Kona in the early twentieth century, she knew nothing about growing coffee. But just as her predecessors persevered, so did her spirit and determination drive her on. She began her farm in 1988.

She used innovative methods, such as using geese for pest control, and became one of Kona's first certified producers of organic coffee.

There were corporate investors who set up shop. The Ueshima Coffee Company (UCC) of Japan, one of the largest distributors of coffee in the world, purchased a Kona coffee farm and began its operations.[13]

Another significant returnee to Kona was Agoot. Born in Hilo, his parents moved to Kona in 1955 and bought a fifteen-acre coffee farm in Hōnaunau, South Kona. Like others who grew up on a coffee farm, Agoot experienced the hard work and the difficult life farmers faced. He recalls harvesting coffee six months of the year—as a picker at early-bearing farms closer to the ocean and on the high-elevation family farm later during the season.[14] He left Kona after his graduation from high school in 1964 and spent much of his working life as a supervisor in the coal mines of Illinois. He returned in the 1980s and rose to become manager of the Pacific Coffee Cooperative.

Like their predecessors, these new farmers were tenacious, hard-working, independent, yet cooperative. Unlike the first- and second-generation farmers, however, these new farmers were outspoken and more sophisticated in ways of doing business. Although many farmers still remained members of the farm cooperatives, many sought new ways of marketing.

Coming Together—A Redux

The quest for pure Kona coffee took a major step forward in 1984 when these newcomers formed the Kona Coffee Council (KCC). The Kona Coffee Association formed in the 1960s had enjoyed some success in establishing the first coffee-grading standards and getting Kona coffee into the gourmet market by way of the contract with the Superior Tea and Coffee Company. The old association was made up of representatives of the various cooperatives and others who were associated with processing. With the decline in the number of mills and with the number of cooperatives reduced to two, most of the original members were no longer active with the industry. While the old organization had made progress, Kona coffee was largely a blended product.

The new KCC aimed to continue promoting Kona coffee and to educate the public about pure Kona. A change from the days of the KCA board, which was made up of millers and co-op representatives, was the number of farmers allowed to serve on the KCC's board of directors. Initially, six of the twelve KCC directors were to be processors, five farmers, and one was a member from the Farm Bureau.[15] This organization remained until the mid-1990s, when the council voted to elect all directors at large. Going into the twenty-first century, the majority of the directors were farmers.[16]

Vertical Integration—The Next Step

Although the sale of Kona coffee as a blend to the general retail market continued, pure Kona was now a reality. Distribution of Kona was through institutions, the export market, the specialty/-gourmet markets, and to residents. Japan loomed as a strong potential market because of their growing consumption of specialty coffee.[17]

The Greenwells and the Twigg-Smiths were among those who took vertical integration to another level by incorporating wet processing, dry milling, and roasting into their operations. They sold pure Kona directly to consumers and to other companies by creating their own markets. They provided processing and roasting services to other growers, enabling them to also enter the direct sales arena. This trend of processing grew, and by the end of the 1980s, there were twenty-one processors in Kona—up from the three that started the decade.[18]

In 1989, Kona enjoyed a $6 per pound price despite the dissolution of an international agreement and lifting of export quotas. By the end of the 1980s there were twenty-seven businesses vying for Kona coffee.[19]

CHAPTER 11

FIGHT FOR IDENTITY

By the 1990s a new type of structure had entered the Kona coffee belt. The new *hoshidana* was built with a translucent plastic roof and did not require opening and closing. Although the old sliding roof was still prominent, the new models were gaining popularity. Harvesting was still a major expense, amounting to 60 to 90 percent of total costs, and a lack of labor prevented expansion.[1] Therefore, many farms turned to foreign countries in search of pickers; soon, Latin America would become a major source of harvest labor.[2]

Norman Greenwell's attempts at solving the labor problem were innovative. He did what many had only talked about in the past, commissioning Hawai'i's first self-propelled mechanical coffee harvester in 1989. Greenwell did not retain the harvester for long and returned to hand picking after realizing his farm was not set up for such a machine. There were many reasons why Greenwell opted to abandon mechanical harvesting. One was the lack of an irrigation system; artificial irrigation aids in reliability of yield, which is necessary for a profitable mechanically harvested operation. The Korvan harvester developed at Greenwell's farm, however, became the prototype for the harvesters used in other parts of Hawai'i.[3]

By 1993, Kona's coffee acreage stood at 1,370, less than a third of what it had been at its peak during the 1930s. Kona had also

An early twenty-first-century *hoshidana* with a plastic sun roof. *(Photograph by Gerald Kinro, 2001.)*

been supplanted by Kaua'i as Hawai'i's coffee groves replaced sugar fields in Kaua'i in the mid-1980s. Kaua'i also boasted innovations such as mechanical harvesters that stripped trees clean. As they had on their sugar plantations, the Kaua'i coffee farmers strove for total efficiency and a wider profit margin. Kona's reduced coffee acreage was not all bad, however. Many of Kona's farmers had diversified into other crops, and many farmed part-time.

Coffee fields also were started on Moloka'i, Maui, and O'ahu. In a repeat of what had taken place in the 1800s, big businesses rushed to enter the coffee market and to capitalize on the good prices of gourmet coffee. Some of the new farmers in other parts of the state were familiar names to Kona. Former sugar giant Castle and Cook began a coffee operation on O'ahu. J.B. Castle, the son of the company's cofounder, once had interests in the Captain Cook Coffee Company. AMFAC, which once dominated Kona coffee as

H. Hackfield Company and as American Factors, began an orchard on Maui. By 1996, there were ten farms on Kaua'i, Maui, O'ahu, and Moloka'i with a total of 4,940 acres and $10 million in sales. Despite its small size, however, Kona's coffee industry was viable. Kona's 550 farms consisted of 1,960 harvested acres that produced a booming $10.8 million in sales.[4]

The Hawai'i Coffee Growers Association (HCGA) was organized in late 1989 and was made up of growers from all islands.[5] HCGA hoped to serve coffeegrowers throughout Hawai'i. Some of its objectives were promoting all Hawai'i coffees, funding research and development, and guiding and supporting good legislation. Many Kona growers were hesitant to join the association, however, feeling their product would be diluted. In 1997 Kona coffee was worth $11 per pound,[6] twice as much as the coffee produced in the rest of the state. Many Kona growers felt that being a part of the HCGA would bring prices down.

Furthermore, the farms in Kona were largely family-run, and growers in other parts of Hawai'i represented big businesses. Kona farmers saw a potential loss of identity; they feared being absorbed and being grouped with growers elsewhere. "I didn't think we had much in common except the word coffee," said Cea Smith, past president of the Kona Coffee Council.[7] In a divided vote, the Kona Coffee Council voted to join the association in 1994, nearly five years after HCGA's inception.

In 1994, competing cooperatives saw little value in being separate. They were having difficult financial times. Therefore, the Kona Farmers Cooperative merged with the Pacific Coffee Cooperative and called itself the Kona Pacific Coffee Cooperative (KPCC). Agoot, the manager of the PCC, was retained to manage the new entity. Like his predecessor, Kudo, Agoot advocated quality. Agoot wanted improved grading standards. He also wanted fair prices for his members and sought out markets for coffee not roasted by KPFC's facility. He also stressed educating the public on the merits of pure Kona coffee.

Processing facilities at the Kona Pacific Farmers Cooperative, once the location of the Captain Cook Coffee Company. *(Photograph by Gerald Kinro, 2001.)*

Despite Kona's reputation for quality, Agoot realized the challenges and the competition he faced. Kona's farmers were subject to stricter government regulations than farmers in other parts of the world. "We are producing a third-world crop under first-world conditions. We have to pay higher costs for labor, taxes and land," he said.[8] Kona farmers had to be more efficient and get the best prices possible; he wanted his farmers to be reliable in quantity and quality. Agoot felt that farmers should irrigate coffee fields. Although Kona's reverse rainfall pattern had served the industry well, droughts were affecting the crop. "Praying is unproved, but fertilizer is only about $3,000 per ton," he said.[9]

The Fight for Pure Kona

Because of the planting of coffee in other parts of the state, Kona growers were concerned about the identity of their product. These concerns were fueled by roasters and other distributors using the

Kona name merely to get better prices. Once coffee left Kona, roasters marketed the product any way they chose, for there was no definition of a *Kona blend.*

The Hawai'i County Council on Economic Development felt that at least 51 percent of a blend should be Kona before it could be considered a Kona blend.[10] Masao Nakamura, vice president of Mauna Loa Macadamia Nut Company, a C. Brewer company that purchased Superior Tea and Coffee, differed sharply. He claimed that consumers didn't want too much Kona in their blends because that would make the coffee too strong. An increase in the amount of Kona in the blend also would drive costs too high.[11] Others felt that abuse of the Kona name would lessen the quality of the coffee.

In response to these arguments and in response to the Kona Coffee Council, the state legislature passed a law that went into effect in 1992. The new statute required blends to be at least 10 percent Kona coffee before they could be marketed as a Kona blend. Many felt this law was watered down and carried the fight onward.

Grower Tom Greenwell considered this weak standard "false advertising" because, he said, it allowed Kona coffee beans to be mixed with low-grade beans, twigs, and other debris. "Technically, it is 100 percent Kona," he said, "but it's stuff I put on my compost pile."[12] Michael Craig, another grower, saw the misuse of the name *Kona* as a misuse of the cultural heritage of Hawai'i.[13]

The identity and reputation of Kona coffee, however, experienced a giant setback in 1996. It was discovered that Michael Norton of the Kona Kai Farms, a Berkeley, California-based distributor, had purchased inferior Panamanian and Costa Rican beans and sold these as Kona coffee at premium prices. The coffee would have sold at one-third to one-fourth that price if marketed honestly. Norton earned more than $15 million through this scheme. According to court papers filed in the U.S. District Court in Northern California, Norton purchased 3.6 million pounds of coffee from a dealer in Costa Rica between 1993 and 1996.[14] Only 1 million pounds of that quantity was Kona. Norton then arranged for another agent to act as a buyer through the Nagoya Company, which Norton funded. He transferred coffee from Central America to bags labeled "Kona Kai Farms-Kealakekua, Hawai'i—Pure Kona Coffee—Product of the USA."[15]

Norton sold coffee several times to a business named Hawaiian Kona Coffee Company. Revenue totaled $1 million for the year 1995. Norton arranged to have the money forwarded to two Hong Kong businesses, which in turn transferred the $1 million to a Swiss bank account.[16]

When an informant in the U.S. Customs Service reported Norton's activities, several agencies stepped in to investigate, including the U.S. Customs Service, the Internal Revenue Service, the Food and Drug Administration, and California authorities.

Norton violated the federal Food and Drug and Cosmetic Act by selling a misbranded product. He was sentenced to two and a half years in a federal prison and was ordered to pay $440,000 in back taxes in March 2002. The government seized $5 million of Norton's assets with about $500,000 going to the twenty-one coffee companies that purchased coffee from Norton.[17]

The real blow was that coffee *cuppers,* or taste-testers, claimed that the inferior grade of coffee Norton sold was better than pure Kona coffee. Prices for Kona coffee fell immediately, and many major distributors stopped purchasing Kona coffee.

As their predecessors had done a generation ago, Kona farmers circled the wagons. They lobbied the state legislature. In response to their concerns, the legislature passed a law that requires certification of Kona coffee. It mandated authentication of origin and grade before shipping.

Another effect of the Kona Kai scandal was the divisiveness it created. A group of growers favored litigation against Kona Kai, saying that the Kona name needed protection. They wished to be compensated for their efforts because all involved were to benefit.

On the other hand, some felt that litigation would further tarnish an already reeling industry. In the end, eighteen growers filed suit. They won a $1 million judgment in civil court; in addition, $225,000 was paid to other defendants. In 2000, the Hawai'i Department of Agriculture received federal certification marks from the U.S. Patent and Trademark Office for coffees grown in Hawai'i, including 100 percent Kona coffee.[18] In another step toward protecting Kona's identity, the Hawai'i legislature passed a bill in 2002 that required coffee packages to list the exact percentage of Kona coffee in a blend.

The movement for pure Kona had been steadily moving forward since the 1960s, when Kudo managed the Sunset Cooperative. No longer did growers do business in the manner of their parents and grandparents. Kunitake, Twigg-Smith, Tom Greenwell, UCC, and others opened coffee retail stores. They borrowed ideas from Napa Valley wineries and catered to the tourism industry. They sold not only coffees, but items of interest to other culinary fields such as cookbooks, food books, coffee serving items, and other cooking utensils.

Like their winery counterparts, some offered tours of their farms and milling and roasting operations, gave complimentary

Bags of pure Kona coffee. *(Photograph by Gerald Kinro, 2001.)*

tastings, and sold pure—not blended—Kona coffee. Others, such as Christian Twigg-Smith, opened bed-and-breakfast inns on their farms. By the start of the twenty-first century, Kona coffee had entered a new era, the era of agritourism.

With the new interest in pure Kona, the Kona Coffee Council, realizing the need for quality, established its estate coffee program. It mandated that coffee be of a certain minimum grade and be grown on a single farm.

The development of the Internet into an effective sales tool also contributed to the pure Kona movement by giving an opportunity for those not aligned with the tourism industry to go pure Kona. Bob and Cea Smith had no processing and roasting facility. Their farm was not accessible to tour buses and conventional vehicles. They had their coffee processed and roasted at a nearby facility. They then marketed their products through their Web site and by mail.

Many of Kona's coffee farmers, however, did not have their own label and Web site. For some, the Kona Pacific Farmers Cooperative (KPFC) remained a viable option. KPFC entered the new era and sold pure Kona on its Web site, using its own label. Entering the twenty-first century, there were more than 100 private coffee labels and more than twenty-seven Web sites.[19] KPFC's membership of 300 of the 600 coffeegrowers in Kona meant that more than half of Kona's coffee farmers were represented by a pure Kona label and a Web site to market their harvest.

Hana Hou—Déjà Vu?

The late 1990s brought another down period as world coffee prices hit all-time lows. Surpluses caused a glut in the world market. Hawai'i was not immune to the coffee cycle, and low prices continued into the twenty-first century. The Waialua Coffee Company, operated by Castle and Cook's Dole Foods Division, found its young operation struggling.[20] The glut in the local and international markets and the high cost of harvesting by hand were hurting the industry. In 2001, Hawai'i's coffee revenues dropped an estimated 23 percent to $18 million.[21] "Same

The twenty-first century saw farmers with their own brands of estate coffee.
(Photograph by Gerald Kinro, 2001.)

beans, same problems," lamented John Hirota, Dole's property manager. "Everybody from Kaua'i to Moloka'i has ended up with huge inventories. Coffee is slow."[22]

One of the reasons for low sales was the drop in the number of tourists, especially from Japan, coming to Hawai'i.[23] These tourists were a prime market for Hawaiian-grown coffee. The attack on the World Trade Center in September 2001 further depressed the tourism industry.

The coffee operation on Moloka'i found a new owner, and AMFAC abandoned its Maui operations in 2001. Dole leased its coffee lands to the Waialua Agricultural Company. The Waialua Company subsequently filed for bankruptcy in 2002. The crash of 100 years ago seemed to be repeating itself.

According to observers, Kona growers fared slightly better than those in the rest of the state. "It's affecting us, but Kona is still doing fairly well," said Calvin Lee, head of market development at the

Hawai'i Department of Agriculture.[24] Specialty growers, especially those in Kona, were less affected than the bulk growers.

Nevertheless, there were Kona farms that were dependent on the tourist trade. Some had tour buses stop at their stores. Some had outlets in malls frequented by visitors. The anthrax mail scares of 2001 also affected many who conducted retail sales over the Internet. Some, like Bob Smith, found that customers had become wary of receiving items through the mail.[25] This generation of Kona coffee farmers fought back. Determined to succeed, Smith considered this a minor inconvenience and found alternate ways of delivering his coffee to his customers.[26]

The fight never ended and never will. As long as there is Kona coffee, its tenders must ride the coffee cycle.

As Kona's coffee industry moved into the twenty-first century, agritourism became popular. A farm display explains coffee processing to visitors. (*Photograph by Gerald Kinro, 2001.*)

PART IV

A CUP OF ALOHA

CHAPTER 12

A CUP OF ALOHA

Kona Mauka, Kona's mountainside, during a drought is belied by its looks. Coffee trees droop, desperate for water, their remaining foliage an anemic yellow. Afternoon trade winds further drain the plants' moisture, creating more thirst and decreasing turgidity. "Floating coffee," its tenders complain, referring to useless parchment shells with no beans inside. No, this does not look like the Kona that produces one of the world's finest coffees.

Agronomists refer to the *permanent wilting point,* the point of moisture stress from which a plant cannot physiologically recover. The Kona coffee plants have never crossed that line, no matter how bad the drought.

The Kona coffee industry has come close to its permanent wilting point many times. Each time Kona coffee has rebounded in defiance of the odds. The fields of coffee that line Māmalahoa Highway are a testament to those who kept the industry alive. The rewards of their efforts are reaped not in Kona alone, but in all Hawai'i. Because of the gourmet market, Kona growers prospered in the early 1980s; growing operations were launched in other parts of the state. There had to be Kona first. Each generation has had to face adversity, and each generation has taken Kona coffee to a higher plane.

Planters started the Kona coffee industry in the mid-1800s, then left to pursue other business interests. With no care or direction, the reputation of Kona coffee declined in the 1860s. Machado believed in the product and built a coffee mill so the beans could be processed. H.N. Greenwell refused to compromise the quality of Kona coffee and reset the bar for standards. During the 1890s, planters such as Hind, Miller, and Brunner gave Kona coffee another start.

Hermann Widemann, Miller, Inaba, and Yokoyama left the legacy of the 'Guatemalan' coffee variety that still sets the standard of Kona coffee. For a brief period during the 1960s, farmers tried a different variety. It is, however, the 'Guatemalan' variety, or "Kona typica," that has endured into the twenty-first century.

The replant die-back decline of coffee could have destroyed the industry. The solution was to graft a "Kona typica" scion onto a resistant rootstock from species *Coffea liberica*. Scientists named this rootstock "Fukunaga" after Edward Fukunaga, the researcher who helped put Kona coffee on the scientific map. It was he who began the pioneering work to find a solution to this decline in the 1950s and who began experiments with a specialized grafting technique onto this rootstock in the 1970s.[1] Furthermore, trees of the Kona coffee belt were pruned to an efficient, smaller size. Much of the credit can go to Fukunaga.

Kudo, Noguchi, and others began the cooperative movement, a new marketing concept for Kona farmers at the time, in the 1950s. They fought for the first coffee-grading standard. Through their efforts, Kona coffee was able to enter the gourmet market that brought better prices. Kudo saw his vision of a unified cooperative effort come to fruition. Entering the twenty-first century, just one cooperative represented Kona farmers, marketing both coffee and macadamia nuts.

Akamatsu helped establish the credit union. Founded from necessity by ten people on a stormy night, the Kona Farmers Credit Union grew to become the Hawai'i Community Credit Union, which entered the new millennium with $175 million in assets, four branches, and 25,000 members. As Yoshio Takashiba, an original credit union member, said: "In 1936, our new credit union saved our coffee farms. And our lives."[2]

In 1938 Morihara led the farmers in the movement that resulted in most of their debts being canceled. Yates, the quiet statesman and community leader for whom the athletic field at Konawaena High School is named, helped funnel needed funds into the community during the Great Depression.

In 1978, 99-year-old Waichi Okano was selected to lead the parade at the Kona Coffee Cultural Festival. He and his wife, Kame, had come a long way since arriving in Nāpōʻopoʻo with $4.40 to begin a life. Each of his eight children was born in a modest coffee home, and he instilled in them the Kona values of hard work, cooperation, and independence. All furthered their educations, and they went on to become business leaders, a nurse, and a cardiac surgeon.[3] One son, Herbert, returned to Kona to carry on the coffee legacy and to touch the hearts and minds of Kona's students as a teacher and counselor at Konawaena High School.

Despite being well into their 90s and 80s, respectively, Waichi and Kame Okano continued working the coffee fields they loved. They worked together to fill a bag when their picking skills and speed had begun to wane. Why continue such difficult work? It had to be a labor of love.

It is people like the Okanos who arguably left the biggest legacy of Kona coffee. They are the ones who bore the brunt of the roughest times and never quit. They rode the coffee cycle through the Great Depression, World War II, and through every boom and bust. They represent the hundreds like them who, against overwhelming odds, kept Kona coffee alive. The growers of the late twentieth and early twenty-first centuries continued the fight for the industry's reputation. They endured the Kona Kai scandal and the resulting price dips.

Perhaps out of frustration, scientist Fukunaga lamented that the Kona farmers were too emotional about their coffee, that they should have given up and done something else.[4] But these are not corporate leaders who farmed from the comforts of a boardroom. These are folks who loved the land and loved the work and loved coffee. It took people with the tenacity of the Kona nightingales that hauled bags of coffee. It took folks with the toughness to play a football game without a coach against a superior opponent, only to get "dirty lickings" and then to come back again and again. It has been *Aloha*—love for the land and the coffee—that kept Kona coffee going.

Kame Okano, after a lifetime of labors, was able to say: "We came to Hawai'i because we heard it was a good place. It turned out to be a good place after all."[5]

Tanima, who farmed past his 100th birthday, agreed. "Kona is paradise," he said.[6] He passionately cared for each coffee plant as if it were a child, often speaking to them. "Why you no grow? You want water?"[7]

. . . A Cup of Aloha.

APPENDICES

Appendix 1

Important Milestones in the History of Kona Coffee

1817: Don Francisco de Paula Marin plants first coffee in Hawai'i. His plantings fail.

1825: John Wilkinson and Chief Boki bring coffee seedlings to Hawai'i from Brazil.

1828: The Reverend Samuel Ruggles plants the first coffee in Kona.

1836: First commercial coffee venture in Hawai'i takes place on the island of Kaua'i. This project fails.

1845: Another coffee venture begins on Kaua'i. In the meantime, other attempts to grow coffee commercially have followed on parts of other islands, including in Kona.

1848: The Great Mahele allows the private ownership of land.

1850: The coffee operation on Kaua'i fails due to lack of labor, flooding, the weather, and the white scale infestation. Coffee in other parts of Hawai'i also becomes infested with white scale, and investors begin turning to sugar.

1860s: Coffee is all but gone in Hawai'i except in Kona and in Hāmakua.

1870: By the 1870s, coffee in Kona is reduced to the uplands and is largely neglected. The reputation of Kona coffee is declining.

1873: Henry N. Greenwell is honored at the World's Fair in Vienna for his excellent coffee, despite the decline of overall Kona coffee quality.

1870s or 1880s: John Gaspar Machado builds the first coffee mill in Nāpōʻopoʻo.

1892: The 'Guatemalan' coffee variety is introduced to Hawaiʻi. It eventually is introduced to Kona and by 1920 becomes the standard-bearer of Kona coffee.

Early 1890s: The Australian ladybird beetle is introduced and successfully controls the white scale. High coffee prices bring investors, and once again coffee is planted throughout Hawaiʻi.

1893: The overthrow of the Hawaiian monarchy makes more land available for coffee plantings.

1897: Hawaiʻi is annexed to the United States and becomes the Territory of Hawaiʻi.

1899: A severe drop in coffee prices causes investors throughout Hawaiʻi to leave coffee. Once again, Kona remains as one of the last bastions of coffee. In Kona many growers sublet farms to smaller growers. The influx of those wanting to farm on their own, most of them Japanese, begins and will continue through the 1920s.

1917: World War I produces a demand for coffee.

1918: A frost in Brazil destroys its coffee crop and causes a world shortage of coffee. Prices rise, starting a boom period.

1920s: With good prices, more people come to Kona to grow coffee. Farmers invest more money in their farms.

1921: Konawaena High School is founded.

1929: The U.S. stock market crashes, which starts the Great Depression. Coffee prices plunge.

1930: The University of Hawaiʻi establishes the agricultural experiment station in Kainaliu.

1932: Kona schools restructure their schedule to enable students to assist with the coffee harvest.

1930s: Debts continue to rise, and coffee prices continue to drop. The situation for Kona coffee is considered desperate.

1936: Kona farmers organize the Kona Farmers' Credit Union.

1938: American Factors agrees to forgo all but 2 percent of farmers' debt.

1941: The United States enters World War II. The Army purchases Kona coffee, and prices begin to rise.

1945: The end of World War II brings steadily increasing coffee prices.

1953: A frost in Brazil destroys much of the country's coffee crop. This causes another shortage and another boom period for Kona coffee.

1955: The first farmer cooperatives are formed.

1956: Research on Kona coffee becomes recognized throughout the world.

1957: Kona records the largest coffee harvest ever—18,496,000 pounds of parchment coffee. After peaking, prices begin to drop, and another period of decline begins.

Late 1950s: A water well is dug, and the installation of municipal water lines begins.

1959: Kona records the highest number of coffee acres harvested at 5,900. Hawai'i becomes a state.

1960s: The tourism industry becomes established in Kona and competes with the coffee farms for labor.

1962: The Kona Coffee Association, made up of millers, is organized to promote Kona coffee.

1963: The first grading standard for Kona coffee is adopted.

1968: Kona schools end the coffee school schedule.

1969: Superior Tea and Coffee purchases the entire Kona coffee crop.

Early 1970s: With low prices, high costs, and a lack of labor, the future appears bleak for coffee. Many predict its demise.

1974: Coffee prices dramatically rise.

1980s: With good prices, Kona coffee attracts new farmers. Some are the children of coffee farmers, and others are newcomers. Farmers enter the specialty coffee market.

1984: The Kona Coffee Council is formed to promote Kona coffee and to educate the public about *pure Kona.*

Mid- to late 1980s: More farmers do their own processing and roasting. With high prices, growers in other parts of Hawai'i turn to coffee.

Early 1990s: Kona is no longer the leader in the number of coffee acres farmed and harvested. Good prices prompt more coffee farms to start in other parts of Hawai'i.

1992: The first standard that defines a *Kona blend* goes into effect. To be marketed with this label, a coffee blend must be 10 percent Kona coffee.

1996: The Kona Kai Scandal is exposed. This results in a certification program for Kona coffee.

Late 1990s: Internet marketing of coffee begins a new avenue of sales.

Late 1990s: World coffee prices fall.

2000s: Coffee in Hawai'i is affected by low prices and decreased tourism. Coffee operations on O'ahu and Maui shut down.

2002: The Hawai'i legislature passes a truth-in-labeling law that is signed by the governor. It requires that coffee packages sold in Hawai'i show the geographical origins of the coffees the package contains and their exact percentages.

APPENDIX 2

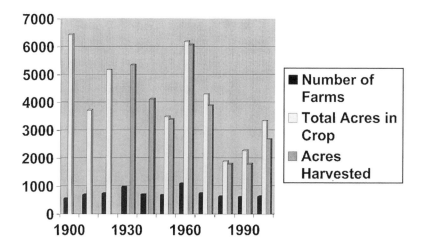

This chart shows the number of coffee farms, total coffee acres, and total acres harvested from 1900 to 2000.*

* Different agencies with different sampling methods obtained the data at various periods. Figures for 1900 include figures from other parts of the Hawaiian Islands. Figures for 2000 include coffee grown in other districts on the Island of Hawai'i. Data for the year 2000 were reported by counties and not broken down further. Nevertheless, this figure shows a positive trend for the Kona coffee industry. Schmitt, Robert C., *Historical Statistics of Hawai'i.* University Press of Hawai'i, 1977, Honolulu, 335; *Statistics of Hawai'i Agriculture* 1946–2001. Honolulu: Hawai'i Agricultural Statistical Service, Honolulu.

APPENDIX 3

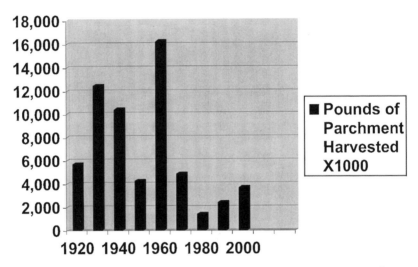

This chart shows the pounds of parchment coffee harvested from 1920 to 2000.*

* Hawai'i Agricultural Statistical Service. Honolulu. Figures for 2000 include coffee grown in other districts of the Island of Hawai'i. Data for that year were reported by counties and not broken down further. Nevertheless, this figure provides a fair picture of the Kona coffee industry. Ralph Elliot. *Hawaiian Coffee, Agricultural Economics Report No. 5.* CTAHR, University of Hawai'i, 1951; *Statistics of Hawai'i Agriculture 1946–2001.*

APPENDIX 4

ABOUT SPECIALTY COFFEE[1]

To lovers of specialty coffees, coffee is more than a pick-me-up drink. Instead of being imbibed for the burst of energy provided by its caffeine content, it is consumed for the flavor and is to be savored and enjoyed. Unique beans and unique locales produce coffees of different flavors, and lovers of specialty coffee will pay premium prices to satisfy their senses. This subject warrants discussion because Kona coffee entered this elite market in the 1980s and has its share of devotees going into the twenty-first century.

Perhaps the most important premise of producing specialty coffee is that it requires the right bean grown in the right place and handled in the right way. No amount of care can make a bad bean good or a good bean better. One mishap along the way, however, can ruin the best of beans.

Good coffee starts with the right variety planted in a particular growing region. Some varieties of *Coffea arabica*, including "Kona typica," are capable of producing good coffee. On the other hand, *Coffea canephora* varieties, also known as the "robustas," do not produce a high enough quality to compete in the specialty market. Once the right variety of coffee is selected, it must be planted and grown in the right area. Some locales, such as

Kona, have a reputation for growing good coffee because of the soil, weather, climate, and other factors.

Once the coffee is grown and harvested, proper processing cannot be overemphasized. Fermenting juices, improper drying, and improper handling are some of the many factors that can ruin a bean. The next step is the grading of green coffee. Some of the factors considered in determining a coffee's grade are bean size, moisture content, color, and weight. Grading programs largely look for *negatives,* or defects. For the connoisseur, however, a great coffee must be more than one without defects; it must be special.

After processing and grading comes roasting. Good roasting is purported to be an art, with the roaster being able to elicit the best from a coffee bean. In roasted coffee, most agree that freshness is essential for specialty coffees. The disagreement among connoisseurs comes in trying to define what is fresh. In order to reach consensus on what is fresh, there must be agreement—that good coffee, well roasted and packaged in conditions that prevent oxidation, will brew up a flavorful cup of coffee.

Finally, the coffee must be ground and brewed. The method of brewing is classified by how the water moves during the process. The flavors obtained from steeping differ from those produced by the drip methods, even when the same coffee is being brewed. All methods—if done correctly—can produce good coffee. Factors affecting success include the size of the coffee grind, the amount of coffee and water, the water temperature, and the preparation of the *coffee bed.* Of course, there is a methodical practice, and it takes time to become a good brewer.

Specialty coffee is, in the end, defined in the cup. It takes many steps to deliver that cup into the coffee lover's hands. Each step is critical. To the thankful coffee lover and to many Kona growers, this care has been well worth it.

NOTES

CHAPTER 1

1. Gregory Dicum and Nina Luttinger. *The Coffee Book*. New York: The New Press, 1999, 2–3.

2. Ibid., 4–10.

3. Ibid.

4. Don Woodrum. *Kona Coffee from Cherry to Cup*. Honolulu: Palapala Press, 1975.

5. H.E. Jacob. *Coffee: The Epic of a Commodity*. Burford Books, 1998, 3–35.

6. Ibid.

7. Woodrum.

8. Jacob.

9. Akemi Kikumura et al. *The Kona Coffee Story—Along the Hawai'i Belt Road*. Los Angeles: Japanese American National Museum, 1995.

10. Woodrum.

11. Jacob.

12. Ibid., 140–143.

13. Ibid.

14. Ibid.

15. Ibid.

16. Ibid., 43.

17. Woodrum.

18. Ross H. Gast. *Don Francisco de Paula Marin.* Honolulu: University of Hawai'i Press for the Hawai'i Historical Society, 1973, 40–57, 136, 137.

19. Ralph Kuykendal. *The Hawaiian Kingdom Volume I: 1778–1854.* Honolulu: University of Hawai'i Press, 1938, 76–79.

20. Woodrum.

21. Gast, 104.

22. Woodrum.

Chapter 2

1. Baron Goto. "Ethnic Groups and the Coffee Industry in Hawai'i." *Hawaiian Journal of History,* 16, 1982, 111–124.

2. Ibid.

3. Don Woodrum. *Kona Coffee from Cherry to Cup.* Honolulu: Palapala Press, 1975.

4. Goto.

5. Mark Twain. *Letters from the Sandwich Islands.* New York: Haskell House, 1972, 147–148.

6. Woodrum.

7. Twain.

8. Goto.

9. Ibid.

10. Ibid.

11. Ibid.

12. Woodrum.

13. John Hind. *A Brief History of Robert Hind's Entry into the Sugar Business.*

14. Ibid.

15. Patti Stratton. "100% Kona Coffee Industry Strengthens—Three Long-Time Processors Lead the Way." *Coffee Times,* Spring/Summer 2001. Accessed on Jan. 27, 2002. http://www.coffeetimes.com/strengthens.html.

16. Anne C. Peterson. "Greenwell's Legacy Remembered at Gathering." *West Hawai'i Today,* Aug. 5, 2001, 14, 15, 16A.

17. Goto.

18. Stratton.

19. Yukiko Kimura. *Issei*. Honolulu: University of Hawai'i Press, 1988, 106.

20. H.C. Bittenbender, N. Kefford, and K.G. Rohrback. *Coffee Industry Analysis No. 3*. Honolulu: College of Tropical Agriculture and Human Resources, University of Hawai'i, 1990.

21. Kimura.

22. Goto.

23. Ibid.

24. Ibid.

25. Woodrum.

26. Kimura.

27. Kikumura et al.

28. Kazo Tanima. *A Social History of Kona, Volume I*. Honolulu: Ethnic Studies and Oral History Project, University of Hawai'i, 1981, 749–789.

29. Kame Okano. *A Social History of Kona, Volume I*. Honolulu: Ethnic Studies and Oral History Project, University of Hawai'i, 1981, 592–626.

30. Gerald Kinro. *The Family Picture Book*. Based on interviews with Hatsue Tashima Kinro and Hagemi Tashima, Honolulu, 1989.

31. Agustina Alvado. *A Social History of Kona, Volume II*. Honolulu: Ethnic Studies and Oral History Project, University of Hawai'i, 1981, 1452–1489.

32. Kimura.

33. Ralph Elliot. *Hawaiian Coffee, Ag. Econ. Report No. 5*. Honolulu: CTAHR, University of Hawai'i, 1951.

CHAPTER 3

1. Gregory Dicum and Nina Luttinger. *The Coffee Book*. New York: The New Press, 1999, pp. 40–43.

2. Y. Baron Goto and Edward T. Fukunaga. *Harvesting and Processing for Top Quality Coffee, Extension Circular 359*.

Hawai'i Institute of Tropical Agriculture and Human Resources, University of Hawai'i, July, 1956.

3. Ibid.

4. Baron Goto. "Ethnic Groups and the Coffee Industry in Hawai'i." *Hawaiian Journal of History,* 16, 1982, 111–124.

5. John Santana. *A Social History of Kona, Volume I.* Honolulu: Ethnic Studies and Oral History Project, University of Hawai'i, 1981, 108.

6. Severo Dinson. *A Social History of Kona, Volume I.* Honolulu: Ethnic Studies and Oral History Project, University of Hawai'i, 1981, 418.

7. Akemi Kikumura et al. *The Kona Coffee Story—Along the Hawai'i Belt Road.* Los Angeles: Japanese American National Museum, 1995.

8. Sherwood Greenwell. *A Social History of Kona, Volume I.* Honolulu: Ethnic Studies and Oral History Project, University of Hawai'i, 1981.

9. Kikumura et al.

10. Ibid.

11. Ibid.

12. Ibid.

13. Minoru Inaba. *A Social History of Kona, Volume I.* Honolulu: Ethnic Studies and Oral History Project, University of Hawai'i, 1981.

14. Minoru Tanouye. *A Social History of Kona, Volume I.* Honolulu: Ethnic Studies and Oral History Project, University of Hawai'i, 1981, 629–661.

15. Ibid.

16. Yoshio Noguchi. *A Social History of Kona, Volume II.* Honolulu: Ethnic Studies and Oral History Project, University of Hawai'i, 1981, 887–910.

17. Kikumura et al.

18. *Guide to Kona Heritage Stores.* The Kona Historical Society.

19. Ibid.

20. Ibid.

21. Usaku Morihara. *A Social History of Kona, Volume II.* Honolulu: Ethnic Studies and Oral History Project, University of Hawai'i, 1981, 841.

22. Ibid.

23. *Guide to Kona Heritage Stores.* The Kona Historical Society.

24. Jiro Nakano. *Kona Echo—A Biography of Dr. Harvey Saburo Hayashi.* Kona: Kona Historical Society, 1990.

25. Ibid.

CHAPTER 4

1. Kame Okano. *A Social History of Kona, Volume I.* Honolulu: Ethnic Studies and Oral History Project, University of Hawai'i, 1981, 592–626.

2. Koji Ariyoshi. "The Tragedy of Kona Coffee." *Honolulu Star Bulletin,* July 26, 1938, 8.

3. Howard Tatsuno. "Good Ol' Days." *Old Time Kona Stories.* Kailua-Kona: Kona Japanese Civic Association, 1998, 42–44.

4. Jean Yoshida Matsuo. "Kona Water." *Old Time Kona Stories.* Kailua-Kona: Kona Japanese Civic Association, 1998, 40–41.

5. Teruo Yoshida. *Mongoose Hekka.* 1988.

6. Ibid.

7. Yosoto Egami. *A Social History of Kona, Volume I.* Honolulu: Ethnic Studies and Oral History Project, University of Hawai'i, 1981, 261–326.

8. Minoru Inaba. *A Social History of Kona, Volume I.* Honolulu: Ethnic Studies and Oral History Project, University of Hawai'i, 1981, 330–408.

9. Akemi Kikumura et al. *The Kona Coffee Story—Along the Hawai'i Belt Road.* Los Angeles: Japanese American National Museum, 1995.

10. William Ishida. *A Social History of Kona, Volume I.* Honolulu: Ethnic Studies and Oral History Project, University of Hawai'i, 1981, 411–463.

11. Kikumura et al.

12. Ibid.

13. Ibid.

14. Ibid.

15. Okano, 591–626.

16. Inaba, 330–408.

17. Koji Ariyoshi. "The Tragedy of Kona Coffee." *Honolulu Star Bulletin,* July 21, 1938, 6.

18. Ibid.

19. Perry F. Philipp. *Diversified Agriculture of Hawai'i.* Honolulu: University of Hawai'i Press, 1953, 112–116.

20. Ariyoshi, July 21, 1938, 6.

21. Philipp, 112–116.

22. Robert C. Schmitt. *Historical Statistics of Hawai'i.* Honolulu: University Press of Hawai'i, 1977, 335.

23. Edwin Kaneko, personal communication, August 14, 2001.

24. Yoshida.

25. Ibid.

26. Kaneko.

27. Inaba, 330–408.

28. Ibid.

29. Ibid.

30. Ibid.

31. *A Social History of Kona, Volume I.* Honolulu: Ethnic Studies and Oral History Project, University of Hawai'i, 1981.

32. Tatsuno, 42–44.

Chapter 5

1. Gregory Dicum and Nina Luttinger. *The Coffee Book.* New York: The New Press, 1999, 58–62.

2. Ibid.

3. Edward Fukunaga. "Coffee." *Twelfth Annual Kona District Fair,* July 1954, 83.

4. Don Woodrum. *Kona Coffee from Cherry to Cup.* Honolulu: Palapala Press, 1975, 25.

5. Shiku Ogura. "Kona Coffee: Past and Present." *Paradise of the Pacific,* July 1957, 19.

6. *Honolulu Star Bulletin,* April 24, 1937. 2.

7. Severo Dinson. *A Social History of Kona, Volume I.* Honolulu: Ethnic Studies and Oral History Project, University of Hawai'i, 1981, 467–505.

8. John Santana. *A Social History of Kona, Volume I.* Honolulu: Ethnic Studies and Oral History Project, University of Hawai'i, 1981, 107–151.

9. Koji Ariyoshi. "The Tragedy of Kona Coffee." *Honolulu Star Bulletin,* July 21, 1938, 6.

10. Ibid., July 18, 1938, 12.

11. Ibid., July 19, 1938, 9.

12. Ibid.

13. John Embree. *Acculturation Among the Japanese of Kona, Hawai'i.* Memoirs of the American Anthropological Association, Supplement to *American Anthropologist,* v. 43, no. 4, pt. 2, no. 59. Menasha, Wisconsin, 1941.

14. Ariyoshi, *The Tragedy,* July 25, 1938, 10.

15. *A Social History of Kona, Volume I.* Honolulu: Ethnic Studies and Oral History Project, University of Hawai'i, 1981, 314.

16. "Our Early History." *Kona Community Federal Credit Union's 50th Anniversary.* October 1986.

17. Ibid.

18. William Ishida. *A Social History of Kona, Volume I.* Honolulu: Ethnic Studies and Oral History Project, University of Hawai'i, 1981, 411–463.

19. Paul Shimizu, ed. *Silver Jubilee Commemoration of the Central Kona Young Men's Association.* Kealakekua, Hawai'i: The Kwanzan Sha Co., Ltd., 1940.

20. Akemi Kikumura et al. *The Kona Coffee Story—Along the Hawai'i Belt Road.* Los Angeles: Japanese American National Museum, 1995.

21. Ariyoshi, *The Tragedy,* July 23, 1938, Sec. 3, 6.

22. Kikumura et al.

23. Koji Ariyoshi. "Coffee Planters Relieved by Reduction of Debts." *Honolulu Star Bulletin*, March 6, 1939.

24. Ariyoshi, *The Tragedy*, July 23, 1938, Sec. 3, 6.

25. Edward Fukunaga. *A Social History of Kona, Volume II*. Honolulu: Ethnic Studies and Oral History Project, University of Hawai'i, 1981, 963–1016.

26. Ibid.

CHAPTER 6

1. Tomie Kawahara Ahn. *100 Years of Excellence*. The Holualoa School Centennial, 1997.

2. Sharon Sakai. "Usaku Morihara." *West Hawai'i Today*, Sept. 29, 1982, 3, 9.

3. Samuel Camp, personal communication, 2002.

4. Akemi Kikumura et al. *The Kona Coffee Story—Along the Hawai'i Belt Road*. Los Angeles: Japanese American National Museum, 1995.

5. "Army Buys Up Entire Kona Coffee Crop." *Honolulu Advertiser*, October 15, 1942, 11.

6. Ibid.

7. Charles W. Kenn. "Boom Times in Kona." *Paradise of the Pacific*, March 1945, 13.

CHAPTER 7

1. Severo Dinson. *A Social History of Kona, Volume I*. Honolulu: Ethnic Studies and Oral History Project, University of Hawai'i, 1981, 467–505.

2. John Santana. *A Social History of Kona, Volume I*. Honolulu: Ethnic Studies and Oral History Project, University of Hawai'i, 1981, 107–151.

3. *Statistics of Hawai'i Agriculture*. Honolulu: Hawai'i Agricultural Statistics Service, 2000.

4. "Growers Elated over High Prices but Uncertain of Future." *Honolulu Star Bulletin*, December 3, 1949, 14.

5. Ibid., November 30, 1949.

6. Andrew Lind. *Kona: A Community of Hawai'i*. Honolulu: A Report for the Board of Education, State of Hawai'i, 1967.

7. Ibid.

8. "Development of Small Farms Envisioned by Bishop Estate." *Honolulu Star Bulletin*, November 10, 1952, 2.

9. Ibid.

10. Edward Fukunaga. "Coffee." *Twelfth Annual Kona District Fair*. July 1954, 67–79.

11. Don Mayo. "Coffee's Parking at Kona." *Honolulu Star Bulletin*, March 13, 1954, 9.

12. Harry Blickhahn. "Hind Plans Expansion of Coffee Operations." *Hilo Tribune Herald*, May 1, 1952, 1–2.

13. Ibid.

14. *A Report on the Coffee Industry of Hawai'i*. Hawai'i State Department of Agriculture, and County of Hawai'i Department of Research and Development, Honolulu, 1974.

15. *Statistics of Hawai'i Agriculture*.

16. Lind.

17. J.H. Beaumont, A.H. Land, and E.T. Fukunaga. "Initial Growth and Yield Response of Coffee Trees to a New System of Pruning." *Proceedings of the American Society for Horticultural Science*, CLXVII, 1956, 270–278, HAES Technical Paper 347.

18. Ibid.

19. Y.B. Goto and E.T. Fukunaga. *Care of the Mature Orchard*. Extension Circular 358, HITAHR, July 1956.

20. Edward Fukunaga. *A Social History of Kona, Volume II*. Honolulu: Ethnic Studies and Oral History Project, University of Hawai'i, 1981, 963–1016.

21. Yoshio Noguchi. *A Social History of Kona, Volume II*. Honolulu: Ethnic Studies and Oral History Project, University of Hawai'i, 1981, 887–910.

22. Ibid.

23. Don Woodrum. *Kona Coffee from Cherry to Cup.* Honolulu: Palapala Press, 1975, 25.

24. "A New Lease on Life For Kona Coffee." *Hawai'i Business and Industry,* XII.6, 1966, 60–67.

25. Ibid.

26. Ibid.

27. Gregory Dicum and Nina Luttinger. *The Coffee Book.* New York: The New Press, 1999, 80–83.

28. *Statistics of Hawai'i Agriculture,* 2000.

CHAPTER 8

1. "Free Warfarin on Menu for Coffee Farm Rats." *Hilo Tribune Herald,* Dec. 18, 1960, 5.

2. Ibid.

3. Ibid.

4. "Instant Kona Coffee on Sale." *Honolulu Star Bulletin,* December 3, 1963, 24.

5. Jack Teehan. "Quality Control Problem for Kona Coffee." *Honolulu Advertiser,* September 26, 1961, A1–A4.

6. "A New Lease on Life For Kona Coffee." *Hawai'i Business and Industry,* XII.6, 1966, 60–67.

7. Ibid.

8. Andrew Lind. *Kona: A Community of Hawai'i.* Honolulu: A Report for the Board of Education, State of Hawai'i, 1967.

9. Ibid.

10. Ibid.

11. Don Horio. "Kona Coffee: Growers Band to Put Industry Back on Its Feet." *Honolulu Star Bulletin,* February 7, 1961, 27.

12. Walter Kunitake, personal communication, August 8, 2001.

13. Ibid.

14. "Registration Marks End of Kona Schedule." *Honolulu Star Bulletin,* August 19, 1969, A-16.

15. Lind.

16. "Kona Coffee Moves into New Age." *Hawai'i Tribune Herald,* July 19, 1970, 18.

CHAPTER 9

1. Harold Baker and Joseph Keeler. *An Economic Report on the Production of Kona Coffee, 1974.* Honolulu: Department of Agricultural and Resource Economics, University of Hawai'i, March 1974.

2. Ibid.

3. Ibid.

4. Ibid.

5. "Councilmen Pledge to Support Coffee." *Honolulu Advertiser,* March 8, 1974, A-6.

6. Ibid.

7. Ibid.

8. Ibid.

9. Ibid.

10. Baker and Keeler.

11. Carl Wright. "Top Price Warms Up Kona Coffee." *Honolulu Star Bulletin,* March 1, 1974, C-7.

12. Gregory Dicum and Nina Luttinger. *The Coffee Book.* New York: The New Press, 1999, 60–63.

13. Don Holly. *The Definition of Specialty Coffee.* Specialty Coffee Association of America. Accessed July 7, 2002. http://www.scaa.org/specialty.cfm.

14. Ibid.

15. Ibid.

CHAPTER 10

1. Sherwood Greenwell. *A Social History of Kona, Volume I.* Honolulu: Ethnic Studies and Oral History Project, University of Hawai'i, 1981, 665–746.

2. Edward Fukunaga. *A Social History of Kona, Volume II.* Honolulu: Ethnic Studies and Oral History Project, University of Hawaiʻi, 1981, 963–1016.

3. Baron Goto. "Ethnic Groups and the Coffee Industry in Hawaiʻi." *Hawaiian Journal of History,* 16, 1982.

4. Yoshio Noguchi. *A Social History of Kona, Volume II.* Honolulu: Ethnic Studies and Oral History Project, University of Hawaiʻi, 1981, 887–910.

5. Kit Smith. "Kona Coffee: Things Are Perking Up." *Honolulu Star Bulletin,* March 7, 1982, E-8.

6. Ibid.

7. Ibid.

8. Walter Kunitake, personal communication, August 8, 2001.

9. Ibid.

10. Robert Smith, personal communication, Sept. 24, 2001.

11. Ibid.

12. "Growing Coffee Not Everyone's Cup of Tea." *Honolulu Star Bulletin,* Oct. 25, 1989, E-1.

13. "Japanese Buy Kona Coffee Farm." *Honolulu Star Bulletin,* November 10, 1989, D-1.

14. Sotero Agoot, personal communication, Aug. 11, 2001.

15. Leta Schooler, personal communication, Nov. 20, 2001.

16. Ibid.

17. Stuart Nakamoto and John Halloran. *Final Report. Markets and Marketing Issues of the Kona Coffee Industry.* Department of Agricultural and Resource Economics, CTAHR, University of Hawaiʻi, July 1989.

18. Nadine Kam. "Gourmet Coffee Colors Kona Green." *Honolulu Star Bulletin,* October 25, 1989, E-1.

19. Ibid.

Chapter 11

1. H.C. Bittenbender, N. Kefford, and K.G. Rohrback. *Coffee Industry Analysis #3.* Honolulu: University of Hawaiʻi, College of Tropical Agriculture and Human Resources, 1990.

2. "A New Generation of Latin Immigrants Harvest Hawai'i's Golden Crop." *Honolulu Star Bulletin*, November 17, 1997, B-1.

3. Steve Hicks, personal communication, July 2, 2002.

4. Andrew Gomes. "Coffee Industry Forms Unsteady Alliance." *Pacific Business News*, October 27, 1997.

5. Bittenbender et al.

6. Gomes.

7. Ibid.

8. Christy L. Cain. "Big Coffee Farm Planned for Kona." *Pacific Business News*, April 23, 2001.

9. Andrew Gomes. "Weak Kona Coffee Crop May Force Prices Up." *Pacific Business News*, September 6, 1996.

10. "Dispute Brewing Over Kona Blends." *Honolulu Star Bulletin*, October 25, 1990, A-1.

11. Ibid.

12. Julie Chao. "Weak Blends Steam Kona Growers." *Honolulu Star Bulletin*, November 25, 1995, B-1.

13. Ibid.

14. Michelle Meadows. "California Man Convicted for Brewing a Coffe Scam." *FDA Consumer*, November–December 2001, 39.

15. Ibid.

16. Ibid.

17. Ibid.

18. "Kona Coffee Wins Protection." *Honolulu Advertiser*, March 23, 2000, B-8.

19. "Big Island Resort Holds Coffee Label and Website Contest." *Pacific Business News*, August 8, 2000.

20. Tino Ramirez. "Waialua Coffee Not Taking Off." *Honolulu Advertiser*, August 13, 2000.

21. *Statistics of Hawai'i Agriculture*, Hawai'i Agricultural Statistics Service, 2002.

22. Dan Nakaso. "Waialua Coffee Parent Files for Bankruptcy." *Honolulu Advertiser*, May 22, 2002.

23. Lyn Danninger. "More Java, Fewer Visitors Hit Coffee Growers." *Honolulu Star Bulletin,* May 30, 2002.

24. Ibid.

25. Robert Smith, personal communication, Sept. 24, 2001.

26. Ibid.

CHAPTER 12

1. H.C. Bittenbender et al. "Fukunaga, a Coffee Rootstock Resistant to the Kona Coffee Root-Knot Nematode." *New Plants for Hawai'i.* Honolulu: Cooperative Extension Service, CTAHR, University of Hawai'i, October 2001, 6.

2. Hawai'i Community Federal Credit Union. *2000 Kona Coffee Cultural Festival.*

3. Herbert Okano, personal communication, Feb. 10, 2002.

4. Edward Fukunaga. *A Social History of Kona, Volume II.* Honolulu: Ethnic Studies and Oral History Project, University of Hawai'i, 1981, 963–1016.

5. Kame Okano. *A Social History of Kona, Volume I.* Honolulu: Ethnic Studies and Oral History Project, University of Hawai'i, 1981, 592–626.

6. Kazo Tanima. *A Social History of Kona, Volume I.* Honolulu: Ethnic Studies and Oral History Project, University of Hawai'i, 1981, 749–789.

7. Akemi Kikumura et al. *The Kona Coffee Story—Along the Hawai'i Belt Road.* Los Angeles: Japanese American National Museum, 1995.

APPENDIX 4

1. Don Holly. *The Definition of Specialty Coffee.* Specialty Coffee Association of America. Accessed July 7, 2002. http://www.scaa.org/specialty.cfm

INDEX

ABOUT THE AUTHOR

Gerald Kinro was born and raised on a coffee farm in Kahaluʻu, Kona. A pesticide specialist with the Hawaiʻi State Department of Agriculture, he is the author of more than a hundred articles on agriculture and other subjects in local, national, and international publications.

University of Hawai'i Press

Production Notes for Kinro / *A Cup of Aloha*

Cover design by Publication Services, Inc.
Interior design by Kelly J. Applegate
Composition by Publication Services, Inc.
Text in Sabon Hawaiian and display type in Weiss
Printing and binding by Versa Press, Inc.
Printed on 60 lb. Text White Opaque